THIS IS A CARLTON BOOK

Design and special photography copyright
© 2000, 2012 Carlton Books Limited
Text copyright © 2000, 2012 Tamsin
Blanchard

First published in 2000.

This edition published in 2012 by
Carlton Books Limited
20 Mortimer Street
London W1T 3JW

10 9 8 7 6 5 4 3 2 1

ISBN 978 1 78097 071 4

Senior Executive Editor: Lisa Dyer
Managing Art Director: Lucy Coley
Picture Researchers: Catherine Costelloe
and Jenny Meredith
Production Controller: Janette Burgin

Printed and bound in Dubai

the *shoe*

best foot forward

Tamsin Blanchard

CARLTON
BOOKS

Introduction 6   **Chapter 1 No Pain, No Gain** 8   The Rise of the Heel 12   Flat Feet 18   Waiting Lists 22

Precious Moments 26   Clump Clump 32   Shoes & Status 36   Kinky Boots 40   Techno 44   21st-century Shoes 50

Chapter 2 The Who's Who of Shoes 54   Shoes on Film 58   The Imelda Syndrome 62   Rock'n'Shoes 64

Chapter 3 The A–Z of Shoes 68   Address Book 158   Index 159   Acknowledgements 160

contents

introduction

Far too many times have I taken taxi rides for just a few hundred metres up the road. Taxi drivers swear and curse; the distances have been perfectly walkable. Any relatively healthy person would have happily jogged without so much as breaking into a light sweat. But to walk would have been unthinkable. No, I do not have a bad case of ingrowing toenails. I simply have two close colleagues with whom I have spent many a Fashion Week who cannot, will not, walk any distance at all, simply because their shoes will not allow it.

Fashion shows are not just an opportunity for designers to show off their collections for the season ahead; they are also the perfect place for fashion journalists, editors, buyers and groupies to show off their shoes. Scan the front row of any show and you will see the most extraordinary collection of footwear, by some of the grandest shoemakers around. The fashion cognoscenti is obsessed with haute heels.

Heels are seductive, and no wonder. They elongate the leg and give the foot a really sexy shape. I once saw the former model Carla Bruni (now Carla Bruni-Sarkozy) spend a 40-minute fitting in bare feet, prettily posing on her toes for the entire duration. Just like Barbie, even without shoes, she was wearing imaginary heels.

While I can see the attraction of heels, I am a comfort queen and hate not being able to run, skip or walk down a street. So although this book is packed with impossible shoe fantasies, and is devoted to my two shoe-obsessed, taxi-bound colleagues, it also offers a few alternatives for those who like to keep their feet a little closer to the ground.

chapter 1
NO **PAIN,** NO **GAIN**

WOMEN HAVE ALWAYS FOUND WAYS OF TORTURING AND DISTORTING THEIR FEET. IN TENTH-CENTURY CHINA, FEET WERE BOUND, AND WERE SUPPOSED TO RESEMBLE GOLDEN LILIES IN THEIR TINY, ORNATELY EMBROIDERED SLIPPERS, WHICH WERE DESIGNED PURELY FOR DECORATION. FEET WOULD BE BOUND BETWEEN THE AGES OF THREE AND FIVE, USUALLY TO STUNT THEIR GROWTH TO A DAINTY 13 CENTIMETRES (5 INCHES). AS PART OF HER DOWRY, A GIRL WOULD MAKE A SERIES OF SHOES THAT WOULD BE GIVEN AWAY AS PRESENTS TO HER NEW IN-LAWS. THE SMALLER THE FOOT, THE MORE PAMPERED AND WEALTHY THE WOMAN. HER FEET WERE A SYMBOL OF HER STATUS AND MEANT THAT NOT ONLY WOULD SHE NEVER WORK, SHE WOULD NEED A SERVANT TO SUPPORT HER WHEN SHE WALKED. FOOT BINDING WAS NOT BANNED UNTIL 1912, BUT CONTINUED IN SOME CIRCLES UNTIL THE 1930S. IN THE TWENTY-FIRST CENTURY, IT IS PERHAPS ODD THAT WOMEN – BOTH IN THE EAST AND THE WEST – CONTINUE TO MAKE IT DIFFICULT FOR THEMSELVES TO WALK BY WEARING HIGH HEELS. THERE MAY STILL BE A SIMILAR PSYCHOLOGY OF WEALTH AND STATUS; THE RICHER YOU ARE, THE HIGHER THE HEELS AND THE MORE LIKELY IT IS THAT YOU ONLY HAVE TO WALK A FEW SHORT, PAINFUL STEPS FROM YOUR LIMO TO YOUR DESTINATION.

WALK TALL IN BARELY-THERE STRAPPY HEELS BY SERGIO ROSSI

the **rise** of the **heel**

The stiletto heel came into vogue in the 1950s when a pair of stiletto court shoes was as essential a part of a woman's wardrobe as her gloves, hat and handbag – preferably all matching. Roger Vivier is credited with popularizing the stiletto heel, thanks to his designs for Christian Dior. Certainly, it was a radical change from the wedge heels of the 1940s. The word 'stiletto' literally means 'sharp dagger', and it is no coincidence that the heel was adopted by femmes fatales both in real life and on the silver screen. The appeal of the stiletto is the contradiction between its apparent fragility and its hard, siren sex appeal. It adds height, pushing the foot on to its toes and making an exaggerated arch and an elongated calf. There is no denying that the thin, spindly heel flatters the shape of the leg, and a well-made high-heeled shoe is supposed to be so expertly engineered that it is comfortable, too.

Shoes with raised heels are by no means a twentieth-century invention, however. Japanese geishas wore wooden geta, which were thonged sandals mounted on two blocks of wood, giving them height and making them walk with a provocative gait. In the 1500s shoes were given extra height by a platform sole called a chopine. They are referred to in Shakespeare's Hamlet: 'Your ladyship is nearer to heaven than when I saw you last, by the altitude of a chopine.' It was during the time of Louis XIV and Marie Antoinette, in seventeenth-century Paris, that the heel (in red if you were a true aristocrat) really

THE LOUIS HEEL SEEMS TAME IN COMPARISON TO TODAY'S SHARP STILETTOS

became a fashion trend, to be continued into the eighteenth century when the footwear and elaborate dress of the French court spread its influence across the rest of Europe. By 1789, however, Josephine Bonaparte was sporting flat shoes. And the most fashionable women across the continent followed suit, wearing their delicate heel-less satin slippers with Empire-line dresses to match. But of course fashion works in reaction to itself and by the mid-nineteenth century Louis heels were back in vogue.

The twentieth century has seen heel heights fluctuate as often as skirt lengths. In the 1940s they were high and wedge-shaped and in the 1950s high and pointy. In the 1960s there were low kitten heels as well as towering stilettos, most famously fetishized by

the British pop artist Allen Jones. The 1970s saw a revival of the 1940s wedge and, of course, the rise and rise of the platform, but it is the 1980s that will be forever linked with the stiletto. Short skirts and high heels are a match made in heaven, especially if the wearer wants to flaunt her sex appeal as well as her power. Chanel heels were, literally, the height of post-feminist fashion. The working girl of the 1980s wore high heels in the boardroom as well as the bedroom. White stilettos and matching clutch bags became the symbol of a generation of high-powered women. But just like the stock market, and property prices, it would all come crashing to the ground by the end of the decade. The stiletto brigade then took to wearing trainers.

There are some women, however, for whom a high heel is as natural as having 10 toes or a leg wax. The ever-fickle world of fashion passes them by as they teeter along on their 7.5 cm (3 in) spikes without a care in the world. They insist that flat shoes are

FOR EXTRA HEIGHT, MANOLO BLAHNIK CREATED THESE POWDER-PINK WEDGES FOR THE HOUSE OF CHRISTIAN DIOR. LEFT, HEELS BY FREE LANCE

THE HEEL IS SYNONYMOUS WITH THE DOMINATRIX, HALF SHOE, HALF DEADLY WEAPON, DRAWN HERE BY ALLEN JONES

uncomfortable, and many osteopaths will agree that their feet and the shape of their spines have been irrevocably altered into high-heel mode. Manolo Blahnik began making shoes in 1971. He has always loved a heel and so have his devotees. So the finely tuned fashion eye would say that the high heel is never out of fashion. Certainly, these days, when no one style of shoe, boot, heel or sole dominates, the most fashionably shod feet have been consistently well-heeled.

Two of the biggest influences on shoes, and fashion itself, have been the phenomenon that is Prada and the rejuvenation of the Gucci label. When Tom Ford rekindled the Gucci flame, he did it with high heels, and every woman who saw them fell instantly in love. Each season, when a new collection is unveiled, shoe fetishists among the assembled crowd of celebrities, press and buyers, crane their necks to see the shape of the shoe and the height of the heel. Ford took the idea of the stiletto one step further in designing metal heels – adding a dangerous frisson by implying that the stilettos really could be used to stab someone in the back.

FINE STRAPS – AND THE RIGHT CHOICE OF STOCKINGS – ADD TO THE ALLURE OF THE HIGH HEEL

TOM FORD'S GUCCI
WOMAN WEARS A STILETTO
MADE OF SHINY METAL

flat feet

What goes up must come down. And even the most foolhardy of heel wearers must have a day off once in a while. There are many women, however, who rarely – if ever – scale the dizzy heights of a 5 or 7 cm (2 or 3 in) heel. They are much happier on the flat. That does not mean to say they do not love their shoes, just that they love their feet, too. Flat shoes are associated with sensible shoes, but the two do not always go together. Take flip-flops. They are not exactly the most comfortable,

FLAT SHOES DO NOT HAVE TO BE SENSIBLE SHOES. A FLAT SANDAL CAN BE JUST AS DELICATE AND STRAPPY AS A HIGH ONE

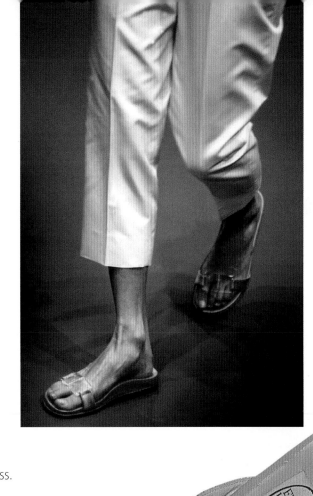

THE LOWLY FLIP-FLOP HAS BEEN RAISED TO GREAT HEIGHTS BY DESIGNERS LIKE EMMA HOPE

or sensible, of shoe designs, with their single thong pushed rudely between two toes, holding the entire sole on to the foot. But in their roughest and most common form, they are the perfect cheap sandals for a beach holiday. They have also been adopted by certain shoe designers as the basis for summer sandals, and often quite fancy ones at that. Jimmy Choo has made flip-flops with a single flower sprouting between the toes while Emma Hope's are fit for an Indian princess.

Occasionally, flat shoes come into fashion. With their gangster look of the late 1980s Dolce & Gabbana made men's lace-ups de rigueur – pinstripe suits are made to be worn with the proper footwear. Rei Kawakubo of Comme des Garçons rarely uses a heel. Her brightly coloured cowboy shoes of autumn/winter 1999–2000 were a great hit with the fashion crowd because they were flat shoes designed to be noticed. In the 1980s shoes by Dr Martens and

loafers by Gucci were as fashionable as killer
stilettos and shoulder pads. In the 1970s there was
the dreaded Jesus sandal, and back in the 1960s
the long, flat winkle-picker was the hit of the
decade. And, of course, there is always the classic
androgynous Katharine Hepburn look – wide flannel
trousers accented with men's brogues.

Many American 'sportswear' companies favour
flats because they are functional and modern.
Donna Karan believes in comfort as well as style;
her Fifth Avenue woman wore flat shoes to travel
to work but might change into a heel when she got
there. The flattest of shoes have to be slippers. In
the late 1990s, there was a trend for wearing
slippers outside the home. Of course, these were
not the common or garden carpet slippers. They
came in the form of elaborately embroidered and
sequined silk slip-ons from Chinatown. Some
designers, including Paul Smith, included them in

their collections. They followed in the footsteps of the Chinese cheongsam Suzy Wong dress and made Chinatowns, from New York to London, prime hunting ground for shoe hounds. Of course, a single pair would not do. Any shoe that costs so little had to be bought in bulk – with a pair in every colour for every conceivable outfit.

SLIPPERS METAMORPHOSED INTO OUTDOOR SHOES IN THE 1990S, EVERY BIT AS FRIVOLOUS AS EMBROIDERED HEELS, ABOVE. RIGHT, CAMPER ADDS A BIT OF WIT AND HUMOUR TO A PAIR OF FLATTIES. THESE MISMATCHED SHOES ARE CALLED 'TWINS'

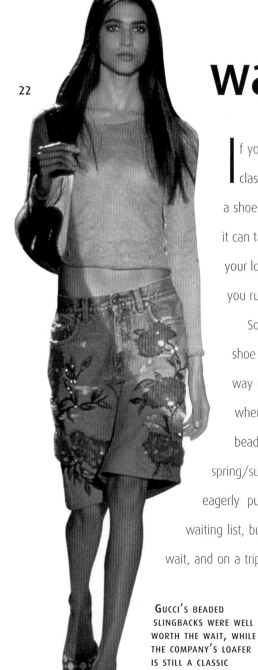

waiting lists

If you have ever joined a waiting list for a pair of shoes, you can safely be classified as a Grade A shoeaholic. You need help. The problem with seeing a shoe on the catwalk, or in a photograph in the next day's newspaper, is that it can take up to six months before the desired objects are on sale. And if, after your long and arduous wait, you do not get to the store on the day of delivery, you run the risk of the only two pairs in your size being sold out.

Some companies limit production of a particular shoe (often a shoe that will feature in their advertising) so that demand way outstrips supply. The result? Near hysteria when stocks run out. Take Gucci's hand-beaded kitten-heel slingbacks from spring/summer 2000. A fashion editor eagerly put her name on the waiting list, but she could not wait, and on a trip to Milan

GUCCI'S BEADED
SLINGBACKS WERE WELL
WORTH THE WAIT, WHILE
THE COMPANY'S LOAFER
IS STILL A CLASSIC

HOW LONG WOULD YOU WAIT FOR A PAIR OF FENDI BOOTS?

at the beginning of the season, she

went into the hallowed Gucci store on via

Montenapoleone to put herself out of her misery.

If the shop had not had her size, she would have bought a

pair two sizes too big. And if she had been allowed to, she would have

bought a pair in every size and colourway. She just had to have them. The

frenzy was fuelled by the thought that production was limited and she may never have the

opportunity to own these shoes again. And what happened to these treasures? Within a very short time, she

had worn them into the ground. Literally. The gorgeous beads fell off and the beautiful turquoise moulded

heel took more than its fair share of mileage. They were then wrapped in tissue and put back into their box

with the hundreds of other pairs of shoes in her spare room, which doubles as a shoe graveyard.

24

The great thing about shoes is that there is always a new style just around the corner – with a brand-new heel or an elegant bit of embellishment to drool over. And, of course, there is always another waiting list to join. Hot on the beaded straps of the Fendi baguette bag was the brand's 'double F' heeled shoe. Before the shoe had even made its way off the runway for the Italian luxury goods house's autumn/winter 2000–01 collection, the fashion pack had put it into their mental shopping baskets.

At Prada, you are guaranteed to find a waiting list for a particular shoe size or style. For autumn/winter 1998–99, it was the leather foliage appliqué shoe which attracted the frenzy – partly because it was a trademark Prada shoe and partly because it was used in the company's advertising. For spring/ summer 2000, it was the kitten heel with photo-print lips and hearts, as well as the crocodile heels in pink, red and purple with handbags to match. Once a customer had bought one, it was hard to resist the other.

PRADA'S THORNY LEAF DESIGN WAS A SIGNATURE OF THE SEASON. TO SECURE THE SHOE, DEDICATED FASHIONISTAS PUT THEIR NAMES ON THE WAITING LIST UP TO A SEASON AHEAD

And for winter 2000–01, the list of buyers was already growing six months before the label's black leather boot was launched. It's a guaranteed sellout, whatever the style. Who knows what styles of footwear people will be waiting for in the future?

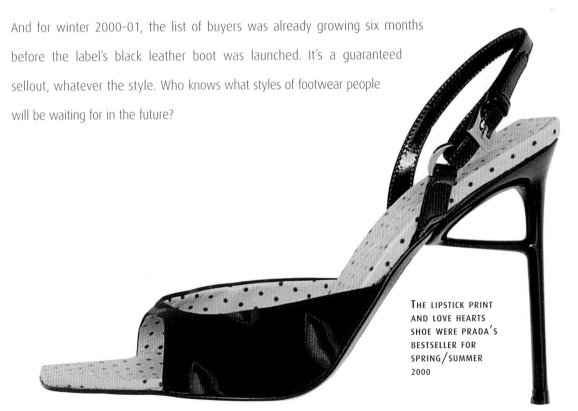

THE LIPSTICK PRINT AND LOVE HEARTS SHOE WERE PRADA'S BESTSELLER FOR SPRING/SUMMER 2000

precious moments

When Antonio Berardi transported the shoes for his spring/summer 1999 collection to the London venue, they travelled with their own personal bodyguard. The previous season, Berardi's collection had been stolen on the street outside his studio, but that was not the only reason. Twelve of the shoe boxes were worth their weight in gold. Literally. These were not so much shoes as jewels, complete with gold chains and straps made from finest 18-carat gold. Backstage at the show they were never let out of sight, counted on to the models' feet and off again. Each pair was worth £8,000.

The gold shoe idea is typical of Berardi. They were made by the master shoemaker Manolo Blahnik, who was also responsible for the wooden clogs decorated with hand-blown Murano glass leaves and flowers from Berardi's spring/summer 1998 collection. But the gold shoes were claimed to be the most expensive shoes ever made. Of course, there are several other claims for this feat, and Gina, the London shoe company, managed to get its most precious shoes into the Guinness Book of Records – a pair of £18,000, hand-crafted alligator mules, finished with white-gold buckles inlaid with 36 Princess-cut diamonds. They claim to have sold a few pairs, too.

FERRAGAMO'S
18-CARAT GOLD SHOE WITH
CARVED HEELS
SET THE TONE FOR
SHOES THAT DOUBLE
AS PRECIOUS JEWELS

MANOLO BLAHNIK'S GOLD
CHAIN SANDAL FOR ANTONIO
BERARDI WAS ACCOMPANIED
TO THE SHOW VENUE BY
A SECURITY GUARD

GINA'S DIAMOND-STUDDED
BUCKLES, RIGHT. MARILYN'S
RUBY RHINESTONE-ENCRUSTED
SHOES, OPPOSITE, DESIGNED
BY FERRAGAMO, WERE SOLD
AT AUCTION IN 1999 FOR
A RECORD $48,300

The idea of shoes as jewellery is not new. In September 1999 a pair of ruby rhinestone-encrusted shoes was sold at Christie's in London for $48,300. The estimate was $4,000–$6,000. The shoes were once the property of Marilyn Monroe and were made for her by Salvatore Ferragamo. Not a centimetre of the red satin shoes was left uncovered by rhinestones, which twinkled in every direction. How could anyone have resisted looking at such precious objects? Especially when they were on the feet of the luscious Ms Monroe. The shoes were bought back by the Ferragamo family, who have since put a reproduction into their collection. But it was not just movie stars who wanted their shoes to be accompanied by a jewellery box and padlock. In 1956 Ferragamo made a pair of 18-carat gold sandals for an Australian client. They cost $1,000 – at that price, perhaps the greatest indulgence a woman could have. But with their intricately carved 9.5 cm (4 in) heels and heavy twisted gold chains at the ankle and across the foot, attached to the sole with tiny bells, the shoes were worth every cent. The sandal is now on display at the Ferragamo collection in Palazzo Feroni. Salvatore Ferragamo also made shoes for Eva Perón. She preferred animal skins to gold and jewels, and the rarer the better.

There is something quite contradictory about wearing a pair of precious shoes. They are, after all, designed to protect the feet from coming into contact with the ground. To wear a pair of shoes worth £9,000 a piece, you risk being mugged and having your shoes unceremoniously removed at knife-point. Such shoes are for teetering from limo to theatre, or from limo to ballroom. The gold Ferragamo sandals look as though they were worn about three times. But then, Marlene Dietrich, another Ferragamo

MANOLO BLAHNIK USED FEATHERS INTRICATELY SEWN TOGETHER FOR THIS SLIPPER, ABOVE. A MIRRORED CATWALK SHOWED OFF DIOR'S AUTUMN/WINTER 2000-01 DIAMANTÉ-ENCRUSTED SOLES, OPPOSITE

customer, never wore her shoes more than twice. With shoes this precious, you would simply want to put them on a pedestal and worship them.

Expensive shoes are a supreme indulgence, but Ferragamo is not the only designer to take them to the height of decadence. Manolo Blahnik had a long-standing collaboration with John Galliano, whose own romantic vision is one that translates perfectly into shoes. Between them, they produced some of the most fantastic and elaborate shoes imaginable. There have been high-heeled, strappy shoe-boots inspired by Masai warriors, all beads and mother-of-pearl buttons. There have been showgirl boots, beaded and sequinned to tell the story of a collection all on their own. The two men also conspired to make some of the most wickedly decadent shoes for the house of Christian Dior: one collection featured platform mules finished with mink, while for autumn/winter 2000–01, there were elegant heels echoing those designed by Roger Vivier for Dior in 1956. The best way to see the design of the shoes from all angles is on a mirror, and for Dior's haute couture spring/summer 2000 show, Galliano presented them on a mirrored catwalk. The backs of the heels were encrusted with glittering diamanté and – here's the really glamorous bit – the soles were diamond-studded too, an idea that both Halston and Valentino also explored.

Diamanté-studded shoes need a special occasion to be shown off (although just wearing them around the house is quite an event in itself). What greater occasion is there than a coronation? When Queen

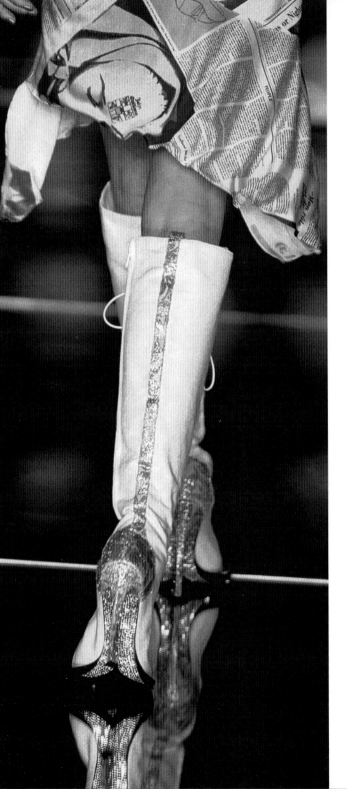

Elizabeth II was crowned in 1953, her shoes were made by the French designer Roger Vivier. They consisted of gold kidskin and were studded with garnets which flashed like rubies, a symbol of her marriage to her country. One French magazine recognized the fine art of Roger Vivier heels in 1962 when it commented: 'Roger Vivier's evening shoes are the works of a jeweller rather than a shoemaker. Only empresses and queens of the screen can indulge in them.'

For many women, however, their most precious shoe moment comes on their wedding day. The famous have particular scope to indulge in such a special-occasion shoe. In 2011, Catherine Middleton was married in Alexander McQueen shoes while the same year Kate Moss wore a pair of customized Godichefac shoes by Manolo Blahnik for her own nuptials. Ironically, wedding shoes – often the most expensive shoes a woman will own – are usually only worn once. They are designed to be as close to Cinderella's glass slippers as possible. These shoes are most certainly not made for walking. Sipping champagne from them is optional.

clump clump

What is it about rebellious teenagers, fashion victims and ugly shoes? There seems to be some strange magnetic attraction. The uglier a shoe, the more likely it is to be a bestseller, even if only for a season. Frankenstein is a big influence on shoe design, as are orthopaedic shoes. The late fashion icon, artist's muse and nightclub host, Leigh Bowery, understood the relationship. His bizarre footwear – one high-rise club foot and one lower platform, worn under a pair of tights – could have been more influential than even he thought possible. The avant-garde French shoe designer Benoit Méléard, whose bright ideas have included the strap-on heel worn in place of a shoe, and the American designer Jeremy Scott, who creates shoes with mismatched heel

BUFFALO BOOTS – THE CHUNKIER AND TRASHIER THE BETTER – WERE THE ONLY STYLE FOR LATE-1990S TEENS AND SPICE GIRLS ALIKE

heights, draw inspiration from Bowery. And you need only look at a gang of teenagers hanging out on a Saturday afternoon, in London, Milan or Tokyo, to see the influence: great hulking trainers mounted on platforms of rubber that reach up to 20 cm (8 in) in height.

At the height of the Frankenstein shoe craze in the late 1990s, Buffalo was the brand to be seen in. The Spice Girls wore them and they became cult items, to be updated almost weekly. There were glitter boots in candy colours, trainers, slip-ons and soles which kept on rising. Even Christian Lacroix joined in the fun in 1996 with his metallic pink and gold trainers on stripy, multicoloured platforms.

The great decade of shoe horrors, however, remains the 1970s, when Gary Glitter, the Bay City Rollers and Elton John all took footwear into another dimension. Nothing was too vulgar, too high, too shiny or too sparkly. Terry de Havilland, the London-based shoe designer, made platforms by stitching patches of brightly coloured leather together to give a handmade, homespun look. If the 1970s super-fly clothes made the wearer look as though she was about to flap her shirt collars and take off, the platforms kept her feet on the ground like lead weights.

1970s HEELS AND PLATFORMS WERE BIG AND CLUNKY

KELE LE ROC'S LOOPY WEDGES

The other 1970s shoe favourite that enjoyed a revival in the late 1990s was the Cornish Pasty. Hush Puppies and Clarks specialized in making spoon-shaped leather shoes that did nothing to disguise thick, exposed seams and extra-wide shoe fittings. They gave new meaning to the Cockney rhyming slang phrase, 'plates of meat'. In the late 1990s the Cornish Pasty enjoyed cult status, with Clarks' seamed desert trek boot being worn by Robbie Williams and Oasis. They were so ugly, they were cool. The same could be said of Birkenstock clogs and sandals, which have spawned many a high-street rip-off. They are anything but sleek and sharp, but fashion groupies love them.

DOLCE & GABBANA, RIGHT.
GERMAN COMPANY TRIPPEN'S
Y2K WOODEN CLOGS, BELOW,
HARK BACK TO TRADITIONAL
FOOTWEAR

Germany has a reputation for producing a certain kind of shoe that is good for the feet and the environment, and just the thing to form a cult following. Trippen is a small company set up by two designers, Angela Spieth and Michael Oehler, in 1992. They wanted to make shoes that mixed high fashion and ecology consciousness and came up with a wood and leather clog. Joop, Yohji Yamamoto and Perry Ellis have all used them on the catwalk. They also developed the sole into a gentle wave that mimicked the form of the foot.

shoes & **status**

Some shoes are little more than an advertising tool. They work on two levels: they have so many logos and signatures on them, they are the equivalent of holding a branded carrier bag. Wherever you walk, they advertise. Customers should, in fact, be paid to wear them. On another level, such shoes are popular; they advertise the fact that the wearer is wealthy (even if the expenditure means that he or she is left eating baked beans for the rest of the month), shrieking money and status from their very soles.

Although the 1980s were regarded as the main era of status dressing, the twenty-first century soon geared up for some serious competition. The collections in early 2000 marked the beginning of logo mania, be it a Louis Vuitton bag or Christian Dior denim boots with repeat CD logos interlocking from ankle to

ADIDAS, HERMÈS AND CHANEL ALL HAVE THEIR OWN SIGNATURES, WHICH SEND OUT SIGNALS TO THOSE IN THE KNOW

knee. Céline scattered its logo over high heels and the Italian house Fendi spread the F-word via its trainers. Even the discreetly low-key French company Hermès had Hs stitched into its sneakers.

The obsession with brand names started in the 1980s when the cult of the designer really exploded. Depending on your preferences for music and fashion, brands meant different things to different people. Three Adidas stripes might have been the coolest logo to wear on your feet for Run DMC and their fans, while the Gucci loafer (and it had to be the real thing) and an upturned collar were all the Sloane Ranger needed to be part of the gang. Put simply, branding is about identifying with a particular style tribe: if you wanted to show that you were wealthy and in the know, a pair of simple two-tone pumps by Chanel would do the trick. There did not even have to be a pair of Cs in sight – if you were part of the gang, or aspired to be part of the gang, those pumps said it all.

The difference between the logo excess of the 1980s and that of the twenty-first century is that, apparently, logo mania is now all about irony. When the hip London designer Luella Bartley wears her

Damier check boots by Louis Vuitton, she wears them with a pair of jeans and an air of utter indifference. She is not so much showing off her status in life as saying, 'Yeah, I'm wearing Louis Vuitton boots. And so what?'

The new branding excesses are all done with tongue firmly in cheek. Or are they? When Li'l Kim wears a pair of Dior denim boots (which were designed by John Galliano with rap stars like her in mind), she is proud of the wealth and the lifestyle they represent, just as the Knightsbridge brat blatantly flaunted her Chanel heels 30 years previously. There is something particularly fabulous, even 'ghetto fabulous', about mixing denim, that most workaday of fabrics, with the glitzy gold initials of a luxury goods company.

As well as linking Cs, gold CDs, Nike swooshes and Adidas stripes, perhaps one of the most potent logos was the single discreet red stripe – all it took to identify a pair of Prada Sport shoes from 50 paces, and a sure-fire indication of somebody

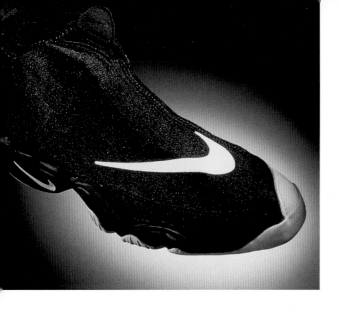

FENDI USES THE INITIAL F EVERYWHERE, EVEN ON ITS ZIPS, OPPOSITE TOP. LONDON DESIGNER LUELLA BARTLEY, OPPOSITE BOTTOM, WEARS LOUIS VUITTON BOOTS WITH A PAIR OF HER OWN JEANS

THE NIKE SWOOSH, LEFT, GIVES THE WEARER A POSITIVE FEELING

JOHN GALLIANO'S SPRING/SUMMER 2000 COLLECTION FOR DIOR MAKES FULL USE OF THE HOUSE'S LOGO TO GIVE THESE DENIM BOOTS, RIGHT, MAXIMUM ATTITUDE

really in the know. You could never be accused of flaunting your wealth with such a simple, graphic device. Nevertheless, the Prada stripe told fellow fashionistas that the wearer was serious about her shoes and willing to spend large chunks of cash to prove it. However, she was a very different animal to the type of woman who flaunted her designer logos outrageously on all she wore. Instead of screaming her allegiance to Prada, she whispers it.

With or without irony, the logo trend has continued well into the twenty-first century. The autumn/winter 2000–01 collection by Karl Lagerfeld for Fendi shrieked designer excess, from the handbags and manicured nails to the flash of metal on the steel heels made from two interlocking Fs. Even the zip echoed the design, a subliminal message that did not let you, or anyone else, forget what label you were wearing. After all, if a woman was to wear a multicoloured fur coat, she needed to dress her feet up a little.

kinky boots

CATWOMAN'S THIGH-HIGH BOOTS, ABOVE, ARE ALL PART OF HER FELINE APPEAL. THE CLASSIC KINKY BOOT, RIGHT, IS BLACK, SHINY AND VERY, VERY HIGH

In fifteenth-century Venice, prostitutes wore ridiculously high platform heels – virtually stilts – so that they would stand tall from the crowd and be noticed. Such shoes would have looked ridiculous on the ordinary woman, but for the prostitute they added a frisson of danger and debauchery. Traditionally, the shoes of a prostitute have marked their profession: high, shiny and very, very pointy, they parody the femininity of a high heel. When transvestites wear high heels, they also like to take them to the max. Like a woman who has a breast enlargement, what is the point of going up one cup size when you can go up three?

Take a look in the shop windows of a red-light district in any city in the world and you will see a range of heels so dangerously high that you can safely conclude they are not designed for walking. Although they are the very opposite of carpet slippers, they are meant to be worn in the bedroom. So, too, 'kinky' boots. So what makes them kinky? The shininess of the leather, usually black or scarlet; the length of the boot itself, usually to the thigh; the laces that tie naughtily up the leg; and, of course, the height of the heel.

As with all forms of extreme dress, the kinky boot has been embraced by the fashion industry and female superheroes alike. Catwoman, who was always something of a male fantasy, wore them. So, too, did Diana Rigg's Emma Peel (or M-Appeal for man appeal) in the 1960s television series *The Avengers*. But the buckles and bondage of the sex industry have been a favourite theme with fashion designers, too. The French designer Thierry Mugler makes no pretence about his inspiration, frequently using leather, rubber, bondage corsetry and kinky boots galore – clothes for drag queens or S&M fashion queens.

The late Gianni Versace's collections were always designed to be worn with high-heeled shoes or boots, with more than a hint of the S&M dominatrix. His entire collection for autumn/winter 1992–93 revolved around the theme of gladiators and bondage. Needless to say, the boots were high and buckled up the leg to above the knee, each buckle fastening with a signature Medusa's head in gold. His highly jewelled and decorated shoes always fetishized the female foot. Gianni's younger sister Donatella, who has taken over the creative control

WHAT COULD BE NAUGHTIER THAN JANE FONDA WITH HER THIGH BOOTS AND GUN?

of the company, was seemingly born and bred in the highest of heels, and she continues the tradition of highly sexed shoes in her collections.

Fellow Italians Sergio Rossi, Gucci and Dolce & Gabbana (whose heels have featured padlocks and chains) have all produced shoes with an indecent amount of warped sex appeal, though it is the British designer Vivienne Westwood who has blurred the lines between sex and fashion most effectively. Throughout her career, Westwood has fetishized her clothes. The 1974 Malcolm McLaren and Vivienne Westwood shop was, after all, simply called SEX. It is an obsession that has been a constant theme in her collections since the days of punk. Along with bondage trousers, there were peephole trousers and the masturbation skirt, as well as a serious amount of shoe fetishization. Her famous elevator platforms hark back to the fifteenth-century Venetian chopine, while her black patent-leather 'penis shoe' of the 1980s made the wearer's foot a walking dildo, a theme Lady Gaga picked up in 2011 when she wore a pair of shoes with Lucite heels shaped as penises for *American Idol*. While a strappy, bright red Sergio Rossi might make a woman look seductively tarty, a Westwood shoe brings out the darker side: the woman who wears these heels is no submissive sex kitten.

MANOLO BLAHNIK'S BOOTS, RIGHT, SAUCILY LACE UP THE BACK. DOLCE & GABBANA'S STRICT BOOTS, OPPOSITE LEFT. VERSACE CAN ALWAYS BE RELIED UPON TO PUT A LITTLE FRISSON INTO ITS FOOTWEAR, OPPOSITE RIGHT

Prada's Sport range sums it up: a fashion collection that takes high-performance sports and the most advanced up-to-the-minute technology as seriously as it takes styling and design. The two feed off each other. Since sportswear and trainer brands have become as desirable as fashion labels, sport and technology have been intertwined. Both sports and fashion brands are striving for the same thing: shoes that are at the cutting edge of design and technology.

techno

The average Nike trainer (sneaker) is made up of 34 different components. It is no longer enough that a sports shoe fits the wearer and is bouncy. It must also offer protection against injury as well as giving the player enhanced performance potential. A trainer does not begin life on a designer's drawing board, but with a team of biomechanics in the research lab. Every shoe is under constant revision to find out how its performance can be improved. Since 1979, when the Nike Tailwind shoe was launched, which featured the first Air gas cushioning in the sole, there have been numerous improvements to the Nike Air technology. Over the years, researchers have developed new ways of adding cushioning to the shoe and more air into the sole. By 1996, with the Max Air, Nike had a shoe whose specifications read more like an airplane than a shoe. By that point, the Air-Sole units, which offered visibility to the gas inside, were as much a feature to show off on the dance floor as on the sports field. Suddenly, it was hip to be a trainer geek and to know your Monkey Paw (a protective device used in basketball footwear) from your Goat Traction (Nike's unique 'dual-density rubber outsole engineered for supreme traction and stability').

TRAINER TECHNOLOGY GIVES THE WEARER ADDED BOUNCE AND FLEXIBILITY ON AND OFF THE SPORTS FIELD

Whether they are Adidas, Nike, New Balance or Puma, shoes that perform well, sell well, especially if they have the endorsement of a cool figure from the sports world.

David Beckham was sponsored to wear his three stripes by Adidas, and Michael Jordan has had his own shoe named after him. In the late 1990s people who did not so much as jog to work in the morning began to buy trainers as their casual shoe. Serious obsessives even took to buying two pairs at once – one to wear and the other to keep shrink-wrapped as a collector's item for the future. The Nike Air Rift, with its split toe, was a classic example of a shoe guaranteed to attract the attention of the serious trainer spotter. Named after the Rift Valley in Kenya, the split toe was, apparently, designed to give runners a powerful push-off. Quite why a trainer fiend like Antonio Berardi needs better performance for 'pushing off' on a run was a mystery, but he – and, it has to be said, trainer fanatics are mostly men – wore them all the same.

NIKE AIR MAX, OPPOSITE, ARE BUILT FOR PERFORMANCE. GUCCI AND PRADA TRAINERS, LEFT AND BELOW, ARE FOR THOSE WITH A PRIVATE GYM

47

It is no wonder that fashion labels wanted a piece of the action. Fendi, Gucci, Donna Karan, Chanel and Hermès have all included trainers as part of their collections. The price tags on some of these shoes make the real thing look like bargain-basement buys. But then, these shoes are about status. No one seriously expects a woman to go spinning or jogging in her quilted Chanel trainers, unless, that is, she happens to be in a gym at some chi-chi hotel in Capri. Prada and Ralph Lauren have gone one step further. They wanted their sports gear to be taken seriously, so they introduced their own Sport labels. Their commitment has paid off; some of their more basic, less fashion-oriented shoes would not look out of place in the more well-heeled gyms. There are also brands that specialize in making trainers for fashion. Australian company Royal Elastics is a prime example. The designers get their inspiration from nightclub dance floors rather than the minutiae of a basketball player's foot movements. Shoes from the company Acupuncture are more about attitude – punk rebellion – and style, rather than performance.

The trainer industry has begun to parody itself. It is no longer a symbol of all that is hip and cutting edge, but all that is utterly mainstream. The trainer has become as universal as denim jeans.

What is interesting, however, is how advanced technology is being applied to everyday footwear, making a new hybrid of shoes that combine function and fashion. Prada took the elements of the trainer – the fabric, the lacing system and the injection-moulded sole – and made them into high heels. These shoes might have been slightly more practical for trotting to catch a bus in than the average pair of stilettos, but running a race in them was not advisable. Hi-tech fabrics like Gore-Tex, Velcro and Neoprene, as well as technological advances in manufacturing, have all played a part in shaping a new generation of footwear.

The relationship works both ways. The Nike Air Moc – an easy, slip-on moccasin that is aerodynamic and features a drawstring and sporty toggle – is the closest sportswear has got to the carpet slipper. So, too, the Aqua sock, made into sharp, urban wear by Donna Karan, who produced her own version. These funny, organic, moulded-to-the-foot shoes are perfect for lounging on a Sunday afternoon, even though they are designed with light hiking and watersports in mind.

ACUPUNCTURE'S STREETWISE SNEAKERS, ABOVE, WERE MORE ABOUT STYLING AND FASHION THAN FUNCTION. THE SPECIFICATIONS FOR A NIKE SOLE, OPPOSITE, WERE ENOUGH TO MAKE TRAINER GEEKS UPDATE THEIR SHOES EVERY SIX WEEKS

21st-century shoes

I f the turn of the nineteenth century was the beginning of the designer shoe, the turn of the twentieth century marked the advent of the DIY shoe. In fashion, there is a trend toward customization and individuality, perhaps as a reaction against the parallel trend toward labels and logos. But this is not the customization of the punk days, when clothes were distressed, written on and safety-pinned by their owners. The customization of the twenty-first century is altogether slicker. Levi wearers could design their own jeans by using an in-store computer programme that allowed them to have their name embroidered on a pocket, or to choose the finish of the denim. Websites, too, like the Norwegian cybercouture.com, allowed shoppers to have

As ØLAND'S INGENIOUS SHOES, LEFT AND RIGHT, CAME IN KIT FORM, TO CUSTOMIZE AS THE WEARER LIKED

an outfit custom-made to fit their own measurements. And Nike.com launched Nike iD, a section of its website which allows customers to design their own trainers. Customers are given a choice of styles and can choose the colour, the sole, the colour of the Nike swoosh, and even give their trainer their own eight-letter ID. This is only the start of a whole new generation of shoe and fashion design which allows the customer to virtually design their own clothes, while offering big corporations the chance to give their customers a service previously only available at small, bespoke companies.

The young Danish innovator As Øland, graduated from London's Royal College of Art in the summer of 2000. She specialized in footwear, but not in the traditional way. Her shoes came in kit form, to be made as the wearer desired. You simply collected different components and clicked them together in whichever configuration you liked. A shoe could be changed according to the weather. 'The whole fashion today is about individuality,' she has said. 'You can put your personality into your shoes.'

The German fashion/art/product designers Bless, whose vac-packed jewellery, fashion and furniture designs was produced in limited editions and sold in only a handful of Europe's hippest boutiques, produced a shoe kit for its sixth project. The components of the kit came from opposite ends of the shoe spectrum: Charles Jourdan for high heels and New Balance for 'techie' trainers. Available in a limited edition of 250, the wearer could experiment as she liked, using her imagination to fuse trainer and high heel, and could play at being a shoe designer.

Perhaps one of the most interesting DIY ideas – simply because it is one that can be mass-produced cheaply and efficiently – is the Japanese designer Issey Miyake's A-POC, an abbreviation for A Piece of Cloth. The idea is that an entire outfit can be cut out of a single ingeniously knitted and perforated cloth. As well as a dress, knickers, bra, bag and socks, the A-POC collection features a futuristic vision of shoes.

While conventional shoes using leather, suede, reptile skins and synthetics will exist as long as there are feet to put in them, there is a move toward ecology and sustainability in shoe design. The German companies Birkenstock, with its cork soles, and Trippen, with its use of renewable wood, have led the way. So, too, has Camper, the Majorcan company, which has made its name with its traditional country shoe made from recycled tyres, canvas and string. One of Camper's most forward-looking designs is the ACS, or Active Compact Shoe, which uses new technology to make a shoe that is light, aerodynamic and, best of all, washable. They are the perfect combination of technology and good sense.

Other shoe brands have also entered the eco-driven

PRADA'S SHOES ARE A HYBRID OF SPORTS TECHNOLOGY AND HIGH-FASHION GLAMOUR

market, such as Worn Again, the company set up by Cyndi Rhoades in 2005 to upcyles textile waste into products such as trainers, clothes and luggage. The first range of shoes was made from prison blankets, ex-military parachutes and suit jackets from Oxfam. Another brand, Vivo Barefoot, one of the pioneers of the 'barefoot' movement, sustainably produces footwear using recycled and locally sourced materials. Simple Shoes' Green Toes is another leader in sustainably produced shoes using recycled and reclaimed materials, such as hemp, car tyres and carpeting.

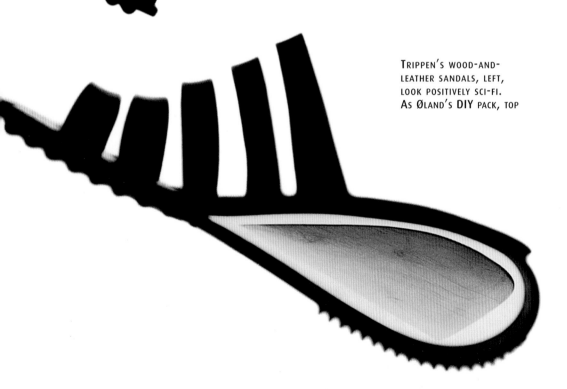

TRIPPEN'S WOOD-AND-LEATHER SANDALS, LEFT, LOOK POSITIVELY SCI-FI. AS ØLAND'S DIY PACK, TOP

chapter 2
THE **WHO'S WHO** OF SHOES

YOUR SHOES SAY A LOT ABOUT WHO YOU ARE. THINK ABOUT YOUR HEADMISTRESS. SHE WAS HARDLY THE SORT OF WOMAN WHO WORE SNAKESKIN SLINGBACKS, NOW, WAS SHE? EVEN ON HER DAYS OFF. AND TAKE A LOOK AT YOUR OWN SHOES. ARE YOU A SENSIBLE, LACE-UP KIND OF GAL? DO YOU FAVOUR HIGH HEELS WITH LOTS OF STRAPS? OR DO YOU LIKE TO SLOUCH ABOUT IN A PAIR OF BIRKENSTOCK CLOGS? THE POINT ABOUT SHOES IS THE SHEER VARIETY AND CHOICE, AND CHANCES ARE THAT YOUR COLLECTION INCLUDES TRAINERS AS WELL AS SOMETHING GOLD AND FANCIFUL THAT YOU HAVE NEVER EVEN WORN.

BUT IT'S NOT JUST WHAT YOU WEAR AND THE WAY YOU WEAR THEM; IT'S HOW YOU STORE THEM, TOO. SOME WOMEN HAVE THE LUXURY OF A SHOE CUPBOARD, DESIGNED SPECIFICALLY FOR THEIR HUNDRED PAIRS. OTHERS HAVE A BOX INTO WHICH THEIR SHOES ARE THROWN AFTER A NIGHT OUT. THEN THERE ARE THOSE WHO KEEP EACH PAIR IN ITS ORIGINAL BOX WITH A POLAROID STUCK ON THE FRONT. A PSYCHOLOGIST WOULD HAVE A FIELD DAY.

IF SHOES SAY SO MUCH ABOUT US, IT'S NO SURPRISE THAT WE ARE FASCINATED BY THE FOOTWEAR OF CELEBRITIES. IT IS THE SHOES OF THE RICH AND FAMOUS – STARS FROM THOSE PARALLEL PLANETS OF HOLLYWOOD, ROCK AND POP – THAT SET TRENDS.

WHAT DO YOUR FREE LANCE WEDGES SAY ABOUT YOU? THEY SAY YOU ARE FUN-LOVING AND GLAMOROUS, BUT STILL HAVE YOUR FEET ON THE GROUND

shoes on film

Just close your eyes, click your heels together and say, 'There's no place like home.' No shoes have played such a starring role in a movie as Dorothy's ruby slippers in *The Wizard of Oz*. They became the shoes to which a whole generation of girls aspired. They had everything – glitter, a heel and a bow on the front. And they were red. One fan in the USA devotes his time to making reproductions and there is no shortage of demand. The image of these shoes remains as powerful today as it did in 1939. In fact, in May 2000, a pair of Dorothy's slippers sold at auction for $450,000. Glitter is always guaranteed to make a girl drool and recent collections prove that it is as popular as ever. Miu Miu's glitter and suede shoes for autumn/

FOR AUTUMN/WINTER 2000, MOSCHINO TOOK *THE WIZARD OF OZ* AS INSPIRATION

winter 2011 were irresistibly sparkly. And when the Italian fashion label Moschino showed a collection inspired by *The Wizard of Oz*, it planted pairs of stripy-stockinged legs around the catwalk theatre, all wearing those ruby slippers. Over 60 years on, it is clear that they are still every girl – and boy's – fantasy shoe.

Children's fairy tales often focus on the heroine's clothing. There was Little Red Riding Hood's cloak and, of course, Cinderella's glass slipper, which has appeared in countless movies, from MGM's 1955 all-singing, all-dancing version to the 1998 *Ever After*, starring Drew Barrymore. The slippers for *Ever After* were designed by Ferragamo who, from the start of his career, divided women into three categories: the Venus type, the Aristocrat type and the Cinderella type. This last, he wrote, 'takes a shoe smaller than a size six' and is a feminine person who loves

NORMA SHEARER'S RED SHOES OF 1948 HAD A LIFE OF THEIR OWN

jewels, furs and being in love. The modern-day Cinders would also, presumably, enjoy wearing Antonio Berardi's wooden clogs with jangling Venetian glass flowers. Especially if they were presented to her on a velvet pillow by her Prince Charming.

The other Hans Christian Andersen fairy tale based around a pair of shoes was *The Red Shoes*, which was made into a movie by Powell and Pressburger in 1948. The shoes in question were a pair of ballet pumps which had a life all of their own and, eventually, forced the heroine to cut off her feet to reclaim her life. In the movie, the red satin ballet shoes take control and she throws herself into the path of an oncoming train. Ballet slippers have long been inspiration to shoe designers, from their chiselled toes to the little bows at the front of flat pumps to the ribbons that tie alluringly up the legs. Christian Louboutin

gave his 'point shoes' heels and grosgrain ribbon, while the flat ballet pump has become a classic.

Other shoes that have appeared on the silver screen have been wanton and alluring. Marilyn Monroe is famously said to have had one heel cut shorter than the other to achieve her exaggerated, swinging hip movements. A painting by British artist Allen Jones was used for the poster for the 1976 movie *Maîtresse*, about a burglar who falls in love with a dominatrix. As always in his work, the shoes are symbolic and

MARILYN MONROE KNEW HOW TO STRUT AND STRIKE A POSE IN A PAIR OF HIGH-HEELED SHOES

highly fetishized. Similarly, the Spanish film-maker Pedro Almodóvar named one of his films *High Heels*, and the poster featured the star, Victoria Abril, in her stilettos, one of which has a smoking gun in place of a heel.

It would not be fair to talk about footwear in film without mentioning Minnie Mouse, the whimsical Walt Disney character who had a penchant for cute shoes. Everybody knows what is meant by 'Minnie Mouse shoes' – the sort little girls like to dress up in, usually their mother's and five sizes too big. Believe it or not, they have been the inspiration for many a shoe designer. The American designer Marc Jacobs used Minnie's ears for his playful, flat winkle-pickers that look like a mouse's face, while Patrick Cox's Minnie Mouse peep-toe sandal for spring/summer 1986 was given a cartoon-like quality with an exaggerated leather bow – round like Minnie's ears – at the ankle. He was inspired by the minimal strokes of Walt's pen when he drew the shoes, and confesses to being something of a child at heart. The roundness of a Disney cartoon shoe is, he says, friendly and encouraging. The shoes also give the wearer a touch of the character herself.

PATRICK COX WAS
INSPIRED BY MINNIE
MOUSE FOR HIS
SPRING/SUMMER 1986
SHOES WITH EARS

the **imelda** syntrome

IMELDA MARCOS, ABOVE,
IN JUST ONE OF HER 160,000
PAIRS OF SHOES. GWYNETH
PALTROW, OPPOSITE, HAS AN
AMAZING COLLECTION OF
'FIERCE' SHOES SHE WEARS
WITH TINY DRESSES, SUCH AS
THE LOUBOUTINS SHOWN HERE

Imelda Marcos has a lot of things to be ashamed of, but her shoe collection is not one of them. She has been a role model to a whole generation of women who have set themselves up in competition with her, all vying to see if they can own as many – if not more – pairs of shoes. The difference, of course, is that on the whole they use their own money to feed their habit rather than that of their fellow citizens. 'I did not have three thousand pairs of shoes, I had one thousand and sixty,' she boasted in 1987. Ten years later, she asked, 'What's wrong with shoes? I collected them because it was like a symbol of thanksgiving and love.' As with any addiction, warped logic will justify anything. Her shoes, she claimed, were 'very simple'. Pumps. It just happened that she could wear a different pair every day for three years.

Shoes bring out the Imelda in a woman. It is a modern-day phenomenon. Like Karl Lagerfeld, who is said to wear a pair of underpants only once before throwing them away, Marlene Dietrich wore her shoes twice, at most. Only the latest style would do. And although Diana, Princess of Wales, was known to have close working relationships with many shoe designers – including Jimmy Choo, who kept the princess well heeled throughout the 1990s – she was by no means the first royal to take more than a passing interest in footwear. The Duchess of Windsor was quite the shoeaholic, ordering from Ferragamo on a regular basis – two-toned shoes for spring and summer, and plain shoes for autumn and winter.

So, who else wears what? You need only glance at the client list of London's Gina shoes to see a who's who of starry feet. The name Gina comes from Gina Lollabrigida. The company was named after the Italian film star when it was launched in 1954. Kate Winslet has ordered Gina shoes, as did Diana, Princess of Wales. Madonna is a fan – on stage and off. Nicole Kidman and Charlize Theron have ordered Gina shoes, along with Kylie Minogue, Britney Spears and Kate Moss. Even the ballerina Darcy Bussell has been known to indulge in Gina. However, she does not have quite the reputation of the prima ballerina before her, Alicia Markova, who took two trunks filled with heels wherever she travelled.

Models have a reputation for collecting shoes. But then, they have better access to the world's most elegant and glamorous shoes than the rest of us. It is not unusual for a model to be spotted wearing a designer prototype as much as a full season before they are put into production. It is one of the perks of the job.

Victoria Beckham has quite a sweet tooth when it comes to shoes, too, and is rarely seen in the same shoes twice. She has confessed to being obsessed with the cat-print Charlotte Olympia shoes that were specially designed for her Victoria by Victoria Beckham collection.

Sex, drugs, rock'n'roll ... and silly shoes. Ever since Elvis and his blue suede shoes, and the Beatles and their winkle-pickers, many popular trends in footwear have started with rock'n'roll. Elvis famously sang about shoes, and his own blue suede brothel-creepers became a symbol of all that was rebellious and teenage in the middle of the twentieth century. The brothel-creepers had thick crepe soles, the forerunner, perhaps, of the Buffalo platforms of the 1990s, and were part of the uniform of the Teddy Boys in the 1950s. Brothel-creepers are still made today and have become a design classic. Saffron, the scarlet-haired singer from the British band Republica rarely performs without hers. Even when invited by Donatella Versace to perform a live set during a Versus show in New York, she refused to don the high heels intended for her black leather 'rock chick' outfit and insisted on wearing her beloved creepers.

rock'n'shoes

In the 1970s P-funk star Bootsy Collins made ridiculous boots into an art form, and Elton John became known as much for his gravity-defying platforms as for his music. To perform in the rock musical *Tommy*, he

continued to play with his trademark by wearing the biggest Dr Marten boots in the world. With every performance his outfit – and shoes – would get more and more extreme. Along with Gary Glitter, who was the leader of the stack-shoe gang, Elton defined a decade of shoes.

In the 1980s girl groups like Bananarama wore Dr Martens. In fact everyone wore Dr Martens. Punks wore them. Mods wore them. Madness made the Camden shoe shop famous for them. Even the soul singer Sade wore them. And then came rap and hip-hop, and the only possible footwear was Adidas.

The relationship between rock stars and fashion designers has become increasingly important. Buffalo shoes were popular with teenagers in the mid-1990s, but when the Spice Girls took to wearing them everywhere, the company could not stack the shelves fast enough with those platform bumper-car shoes. Gina's collection for autumn/winter 2000–01 was called Rock Star and featured boots for evening in fabrics like shiny python skin and embossed velvet, and with heels encrusted with jewels. No wonder Tina Turner, Skin from Skunk Anansie and Jennifer Lopez all shopped there. Madonna wore hers for the video of 'American Pie'. Singers like Lauryn Hill and Missie Elliott were the fashion icons of their day and John Galliano certainly thought so. Galliano dedicated a collection to Foxy Brown and Ms Hill, making knee-high, distressed denim boots for Christian Dior with the music queens in mind. He has taken music subcultures as his reference point for other collections, starting with rock'n'roll bobby soxers and their stilettos, taking in punks with bondage boots, two-tone mods with winkle-pickers and even a nod toward Leigh Bowery and the excesses of the 1980s London club scene. Even Rei Kawakubo has been known to come over all punk, with leather bondage boots.

Dolce & Gabbana and Gucci have both cultivated the music scene: D&G with Madonna and Gucci's Tom Ford paying homage to Cher. But Versace was the label for the rock glitterati. The Versace book *Rock and Royalty* makes little differentiation between Prince Charles and, well, Prince. Except that Prince, the artist, wears a pair of purple pixie boots with a high heel and a side zip. If you want to look – and feel – like a rock star, a pair of snakeskin heels or something with a diamanté buckle is all you need. Sandy Shaw, of course, made a virtue of wearing no shoes at all.

LAURYN HILL, OPPOSITE LEFT, ALWAYS LOOKS COOL, FROM HER HEAD TO HER FEET; MADONNA, OPPOSITE RIGHT, SAYS HER MANOLOS LAST MUCH LONGER THAN SEX; SANDIE SHAW, BELOW, ALWAYS PREFERRED TO GO BAREFOOT

chapter 3
THE **A–Z** OF SHOES

THERE ARE SOME WOMEN WHO FILE THEIR SHOE COLLECTIONS ALPHABETICALLY. THEY MIGHT BEGIN AT 'B' FOR BLAHNIK (THE SORT OF WOMAN WHO GOES TO THESE LENGTHS HAS SO MANY BLAHNIKS YOU WOULD THINK SHE WAS A CENTIPEDE) AND END AT 'V' FOR VIVIER. THEY ARE LOVINGLY STORED IN BOXES WITH A LABEL FOR EASY VIEWING. WHEN SHE HAS ONLY HALF AN HOUR TO GET DRESSED TO GO OUT FOR AN EVENING AT A CLUB OR RESTAURANT, IT'S IMPORTANT THAT SHE CAN ACCESS HER HUGE COLLECTION OF SHOES AS QUICKLY AND EFFICIENTLY AS POSSIBLE. THE REAL SHOE LOVER IS AS FANATICAL ABOUT HER SHOES AS HER PARTNER MIGHT BE ABOUT HIS MUSIC COLLECTION. EVEN IF THE SHOES ARE NOT CATALOGUED BY DESIGNER, IT WOULD BE UNHEARD OF SIMPLY TO LEAVE THEM IN A PILE UNDER THE BED. SHOES, YOU SEE, MUST BE TREATED WITH THE UTMOST RESPECT. SO WHAT WILL IT BE? 'G' FOR GUCCI? 'L' FOR LOUBOUTIN OR 'P' FOR PRADA? HAPPY FILING.

AZZEDINE ALAÏA

When Azzedine Alaïa presented a rare haute couture collection during the Paris fashion shows of July 2011, only a handful of fashion editors, loyal customers and friends of the designer were invited. Alaïa famously refuses to play the fashion game and shows his collections when he chooses to, and his guest lists are entirely hand-picked. Donatella Versace was invited, as was Kanye West and Sofia Coppola. Among the Alaïa cognoscenti who swear by his incredibly crafted, clingy dresses that pull in and support all the right places are Michelle Obama, Carla Bruni-Sarkozy, Madonna, Victoria Beckham (who would probably wear Alaïa over her own designs) and Naomi Campbell, with whom he has worked with and supported since she started modelling as a teenager.

Alaïa, whose label was launched in 1983, is a living legend, a master craftsman who is happiest working into the night in the atelier in the Marais where he also lives, perfecting the cut of every single item of clothing he produces. Born in 1940 in Tunisia, he studied sculpture at the École des Beaux-Arts in Tunis and moved to Paris in 1957 to work with Christian Dior

before working for Guy Laroche and then Thierry Mugler. Alaïa opened his own atelier, making private orders for his loyal jetset following in the late 1970s. Grace Jones was – and still is – a friend and fan, as was Greta Garbo.

Not surprisingly, Alaïa's shoes are equally sought after. He is the fashionista's designer of choice – the insider's not-so secret secret. Such is the draw of his shoes – with their exquisite heels, their strappy lacing, their studded decorations, animal-print calf skins, perforated leather and immaculate wedges – that fans will regularly buy a style in every colourway.

RED OPEN-TOE SHOE-BOOTS FROM SPRING/SUMMER 2011, ABOVE, WERE ALSO AVAILABLE IN CROCODILE. SEXY LACING ON BLACK ALAÏA HEELS, OPPOSITE

BRIAN ATWOOD

The American designer Brian Atwood launched his own shoe label in 2001. His beautifully balanced designs are the result of a training in art and architecture before he focused his attention on fashion at the Fashion Institute of Technology in New York. Unusually, Atwood worked as a model for seven years before being hired by Gianni Versace to work at Versus. After becoming head of accessories for Versace, where he learnt the intricacies of the best Italian craftsmen for eight years, he set out to create his own line.

Atwood understood the sex appeal of the shoe as well as the importance of craft – a winning combination – and he quickly established a loyal clientele of Hollywood celebrities including Scarlett Johansson, Victoria Beckham, Demi Moore, Madonna, Gwyneth Paltrow, Sarah Jessica Parker and Nicole Kidman, who loved the way his shoes made them look and feel. In 2003, he won the CFDA (Council of Fashion Designers of America) Swarovski's Perry Ellis Award for best accessory design. Then, in 2007, he was made creative director of the classic Swiss show brand, Bally, but he left after his autumn/winter 2010 collection.

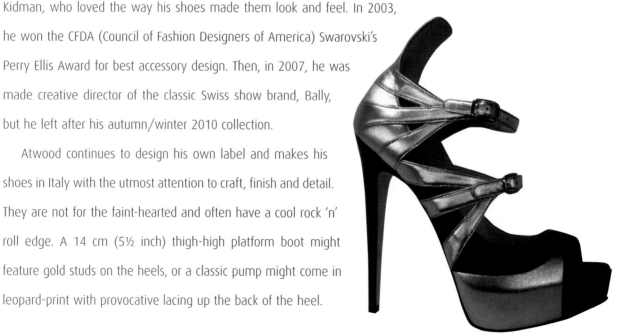

Atwood continues to design his own label and makes his shoes in Italy with the utmost attention to craft, finish and detail. They are not for the faint-hearted and often have a cool rock 'n' roll edge. A 14 cm (5½ inch) thigh-high platform boot might feature gold studs on the heels, or a classic pump might come in leopard-print with provocative lacing up the back of the heel.

A SELECTION OF ATWOOD STYLES, CLOCKWISE FROM RIGHT: JOSEPHINE, ALEXA, DIONNE, FIGHTER, PAZZA AND ASIA

BRIAN ATWOOD'S FIRE SHOE.
A SIMILAR MODEL IN PINK IS
CALLED FLAME

BIRKENSTOCK

The Birkenstock story begins in 1754, when Johann Adam Birkenstock was born in Germany. Registered in the Church archives as 'citizen and shoemaker', he was first in a long line of cobblers. In 1896 Konrad Birkenstock produced footbed soles specially designed to cradle and nurture the foot and he also created orthopaedic footwear for soldiers wounded in the First World War. Konrad, Jr, joined the company in 1925 and bought a larger factory to produce the Blue Footbed around the clock to meet European demand. By the 1940s the BIrkenstock name was synonymous with foot health and was supported by leading doctors. In 1969 the cork sole was produced and the Birkenstock sandal also became a fashion statement, albeit a hippie one. Birkenstock continued to grow, and in the 1990s the clog was favoured by fashion groupies, art school students and nightclubbers. Affectionately known as the 'Birkie', it is considered an eco-friendly, functional design classic. Thongs, sandals and clogs were made in bright colours and different fabrics. By the mid-1990s the clog was widely copied and even the plastic gardening shoe became cult footwear. American designer Narciso Rodriguez asked Birkenstock to produce cashmere clogs for his first own-name luxurious collection. For once, there's a fashion shoe that's good for your feet.

BIRKENSTOCK'S TRADEMARK IS ITS
REVOLUTIONARY FOOTBED, DESIGNED
FOR MAXIMUM COMFORT

MANOLO BLAHNIK

Just one single word is all it takes: Manolo. There is no need for a last name, no need to ask Manolo *who*? Manolo is quite simply the last name in luxury shoes. His would be the name inside Cinderella's shoes. His is the name inside the shoes of most of the world's princesses and celebrities. Mention the name Manolo and you conjure up images of elegant high-heeled slippers, the sort of shoes that were never made for walking. These shoes come with a built-in bill for a limo and chauffeur, or at least a taxi

THIS STRIPY-HEEL MULE IS TYPICAL OF MANOLO BLAHNIK'S EFFORTLESS WIT AND ELEGANCE

A ZEBRA-PRINT GLADIATOR SANDAL, LEFT, BY MANOLO BLAHNIK, FOR BRITISH DESIGN DUO CLEMENTS RIBEIRO. ANOTHER EXAMPLE OF BLAHNIK'S EYE FOR LUXURY, RIGHT

and driver wherever you go. They are too good for walking, too grand to risk getting wet in the rain, to push a shopping cart around a supermarket, or to scuff on harsh city streets – although there are women who do all of this and more in their Manolos. They are designed to be worn on antique carpets, or simply dangling from the toes of a fashion editor seated in the front row at a show. No self-respecting lover of shoes would be without a pair. Even if they are beyond your budget; there are always the sales, and if your size has already sold out, there are banks to rob.

Manolo Blahnik was born in 1942 in the Canary Islands. He is part Spanish, part Czech (hence the exotic name) and was born to create. He says that if it had not been shoes, he would have created hats, or art, or sculpture, or fashion. Thankfully for his fans the world over, he fell into the craft of shoemaking. He moved to London in

Style. Senso. Winter 1978

MANOLO BLAHNIK'S SKETCHES, LEFT AND OPPOSITE, ARE SO FULL OF LIFE AND COLOUR THEY ARE USED IN HIS ADVERTISING. A PAIR SANDALS THAT LACE UP THE LEG, RIGHT, FOR CLEMENTS RIBEIRO

1972 and made his first shoes for the designer Ossie Clark in that year. His flagship store remains on Old Church Street in London, where he still makes the last (the wood or metal form on which every shoe or boot is fashioned) of every shoe that bares his name. In addition to his own collection, he has made shoes for a whole host of design houses, including John Galliano, Christian Dior, Antonio Berardi, and Clements Ribeiro. For Dior, he created the most fabulous high-heel shoes, encrusted with 'diamonds' inside their heels. The mirrored catwalk was made to show off the underneath of the shoes, which were as luxurious as the uppers. For Antonio Berardi, he created shoes made of goldthat had to travel to the show venue with a security guard. And for a Clements Ribeiro collection, he created a series of shoes covered in sparkling glitter. Madonna remains a loyal fan, saying that his shoes are wonderful because they 'last longer than sex'.

CAMPER

In 1975 the Majorcan family-run shoe company began to manufacture Camaleón, a rough-and-ready shoe that was already part of the local landscape and culture. A collection mainstay, it has been produced since the early 1900s by Majorcan countrymen. Truck tyres were used for soles, stitched on to a basic canvas upper with hemp thread, with string for laces. A design classic, Camaleón is ecologically sound and uses recycled materials. Utterly practical, the shoes were at first delivered wrapped in newspaper; today they arrive in canvas drawstring bags. Later, shoes were made of leftover leather scraps. Camper's soles are still created from recycled tyres, and the simplicity of the designs is unchanged.

From the 1970s the Camper shoe

CAMPER HAS ATTRACTED CELEBRITIES WHO LIKE ITS FUNKY, FUNCTIONAL FOOTWEAR

company expanded internationally and among their hip clientele were the Gallagher brothers. Renowned graphic designer Neville Brody was also appointed art director. Brilliantly designed, each store is a totally different environment, with shoes displayed so that they can be picked up and admired without any pressure to try them on. London's first store, which opened in Covent Garden in 1995, was an industrial affair of cool stainless steel, while a tiny New Bond Street branch once featured a Velcro wall designed so that shoes could easily be pulled off. Camper's designers focus on trendsetting shoes. The Mix line used state-of-the-art fabrics such as bulletproof Kevlar, while Twins featured odd shoes, mismatched laces or different heels. Cartujano used traditional shoemaking and leather crafts of southern Spain, usually reserved for all things equestrian.

CAMPER'S SHOES STAND OUT BECAUSE OF THEIR ODDBALL DESIGNS, INCLUDING THE TWINS LINE OF MISMATCHING SHOES. THE STORES ALL HAVE DIFFERENT DESIGNS, TOO, MAKING BUYING SHOES AT CAMPER AS MUCH FUN AS ACTUALLY WEARING THE SHOES

CHANEL

Think Chanel and you will most likely imagine the classic tweed suit that Coco Chanel designed in the 1920s and which Karl Lagerfeld still manages to make modern today. You will think of Chanel No. 5, one of the most successful perfumes of all time. And you may also conjure up the two-tone slingback pumps that are designed to elongate the leg, to be discreet and comfortable, and never date.

KARL LAGERFELD'S
SHOES FOR CHANEL
RANGE FROM CHIC,
ELEGANT HEELS FOR
THE STYLISH BUSINESS-
WOMAN TO QUILTED
BIKER BOOTS FOR THE
FASHION VICTIM

These elegant shoes became symbolic of the designer

1980s, but have survived to be worn in the twenty-first

century. They are undeniably Chanel and have been copied

in chain stores everywhere. Since Karl Lagerfeld took over as

head designer in 1983, he has played incessantly with the

Chanel logo and its trademark designs. Footwear has been given

the full treatment, too. Lagerfeld has made quilted biker boots, prim navy-and-white pumps, flip-flops

decorated with the classic gold chains, high heels embellished with the signature camellia, trainers,

futuristic Star Trek sandals, moon boots and even galoshes, Chanel style, in Day-Glo pink.

JIMMY CHOO

Malaysian-born designer Jimmy Choo

began creating shoes in 1986, refined
his celebrity shoes at a rather
unglamorous north London
studio. He often appeared in
Vogue magazine, where his
heels were elegant and high, and his flats casual but stylish.
He designed and produced countless pairs of shoes for the
late Diana, Princess of Wales, which were suitable
for every occasion, from the glitziest to the most
businesslike and created shoes to
match her outfits, making sure
they were always
comfortable, never
too high and,
above all,
elegant. Diana

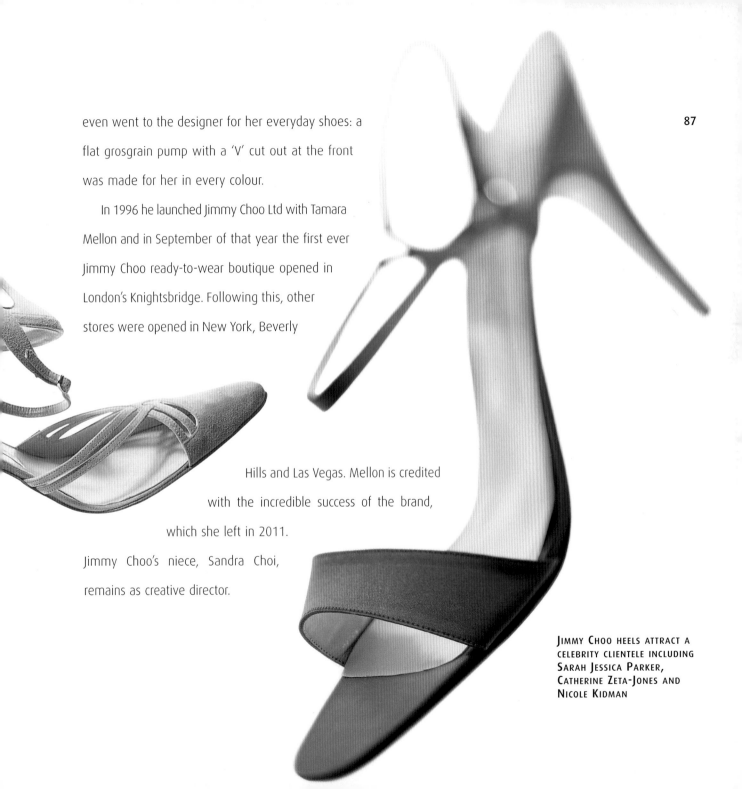

even went to the designer for her everyday shoes: a flat grosgrain pump with a 'V' cut out at the front was made for her in every colour.

In 1996 he launched Jimmy Choo Ltd with Tamara Mellon and in September of that year the first ever Jimmy Choo ready-to-wear boutique opened in London's Knightsbridge. Following this, other stores were opened in New York, Beverly Hills and Las Vegas. Mellon is credited with the incredible success of the brand, which she left in 2011. Jimmy Choo's niece, Sandra Choi, remains as creative director.

JIMMY CHOO HEELS ATTRACT A CELEBRITY CLIENTELE INCLUDING SARAH JESSICA PARKER, CATHERINE ZETA-JONES AND NICOLE KIDMAN

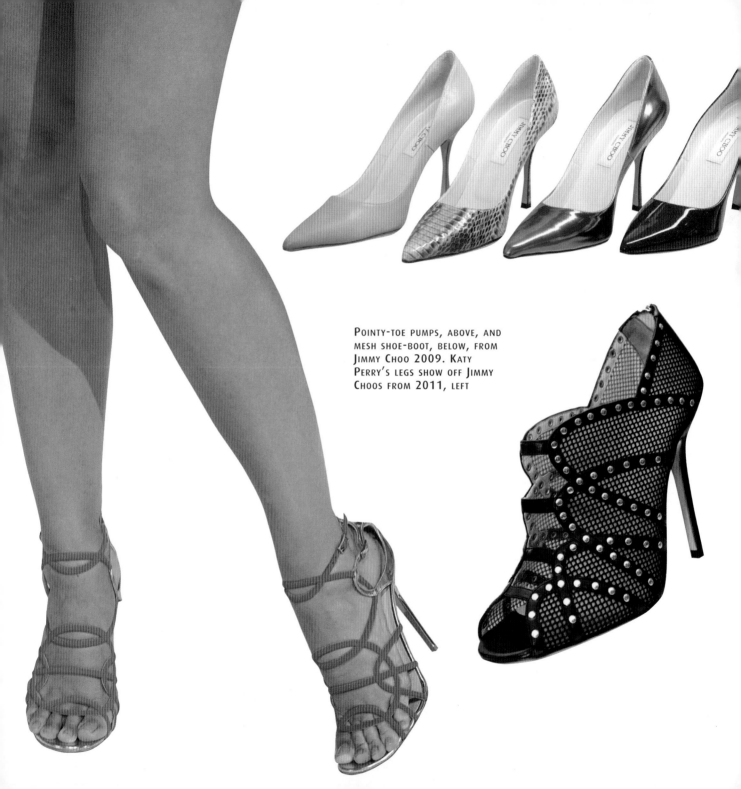

POINTY-TOE PUMPS, ABOVE, AND
MESH SHOE-BOOT, BELOW, FROM
JIMMY CHOO 2009. KATY
PERRY'S LEGS SHOW OFF JIMMY
CHOOS FROM 2011, LEFT

CLARKS

An all-time classic, the Clarks' Desert Boot was designed in 1945 by Nathan Clark while he was serving in the army in the Sahara desert. Clark had seen officers wearing crepe-soled boots (sold in the Cairo bazaar) which were suitable for the hot, dry, sandy conditions. In 1950 he launched the Desert (an instant hit) at the Chicago Shoe Fair. Part of the student beatnik brigade uniform in Europe, it was quickly adopted in the US as the cool man's casual shoe of choice and was worn by Andy Warhol. A recognized footwear icon, the style remains unchanged. The Desert Boot and the Wallabee, another design first introduced in 1965, have achieved international cult status. The Wallabee, acclaimed as 'the world's ugliest shoe' by Blakes in Los Angeles, has been adopted by West Coast rap artists, the Wu Tang Clan, who customize theirs. Based in Somerset, England, Clarks continues to make middle-of-the-road, mass-market shoes for their loyal customers, but the original Desert Boot deserves its place in New York's Metropolitan Museum of Art.

CLARKS' DESERT BOOT IS OVER HALF A CENTURY OLD BUT LOOKS AS MODERN TODAY AS IT DID ORIGINALLY

DR MARTENS

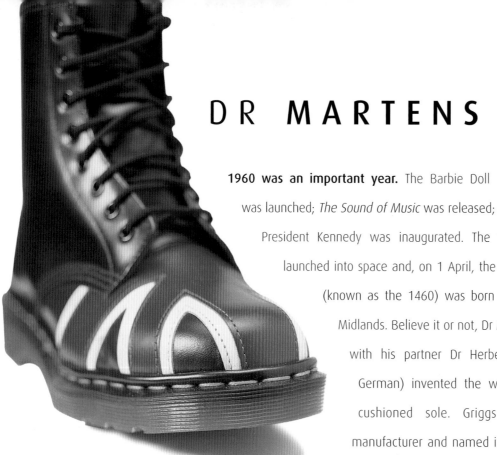

1960 was an important year. The Barbie Doll was launched; *The Sound of Music* was released; President Kennedy was inaugurated. The first weather satellite was launched into space and, on 1 April, the bestselling Dr Martens boot (known as the 1460) was born in Wollaston in the English Midlands. Believe it or not, Dr Martens really existed, along with his partner Dr Herbert Funck. Dr Maertens (a German) invented the world's first heat-sealed, air-cushioned sole. Griggs became the exclusive manufacturer and named it (without the first 'e') after the inventor. Known as 'bovver boots', long-lasting, affordable Dr Martens became a symbol of aggression and antisocial behaviour. They were adopted

THE DR MARTENS BRAND DEVELOPED FROM WORKWEAR INTO A FASHION ICON OF THE LATE TWENTIETH CENTURY

by 1960s Mods, 1970s skinheads, 1980s art students and indie kids, as well as almost every subculture known to man, from punks to hippies, who painted them in rainbow colours and added brightly coloured laces. In Japan they have achieved cult status. Dr Martens continue to be worn in workplaces around the world. In 2010, 50 years since its inception, the 14-hole black leather boot won a fashion award for the 'best counter-cultural footwear of the decade'.

DR SCHOLL

In a similar way to Birkenstock clogs and Dr Martens boots, Dr Scholl's exercise sandals have slipped into the unlikely role of fashion icon without any effort at all. The sandals were never intended to be anything more than wooden-soled shoes, which were designed to exercise all your calf muscles while you did the housework or

A STILL-STRONG FAVOURITE FROM THE 1960S AND 1970S, DR SCHOLL'S SANDALS ARE ACTUALLY GOOD FOR YOU — THEY EXERCISE YOUR LEG MUSCLES AS YOU WALK

walked to the local store. The unique appeal of the Dr Scholl exercise sandal lies in its very frumpiness. It was invented by Dr William Scholl in Chicago in 1962 and was sold, along with cough mixtures, support hose and aspirins, in drugstores.

The main market for the shoes throughout the 1960s and 1970s was housewives and waitresses, who thought they might as well exercise their leg muscles as they worked. Dr Scholls also had a certain hippie appeal since they were simple, low-tech and inexpensive. In 1994 American designers Isaac Mizrahi and Michael Kors took the Dr Scholl onto the international catwalks and even Gap put their own copycat version into production. In the twenty-first century so far, the original design has been released in a variety of finishes and colours, such as snakeskin, metallics, florals, animal prints and camouflage, as well as in platform styles. Although they have largely been usurped by FitFlops and other exercise-as-you-walk footwear in the popularity stakes, nothing quite beats the real thing.

DOLCE & GABBANA

For Italian design duo Dolce & Gabbana, shoes are an extension of their overall vision for every collection. If the collection that year features shiny hologram fabric dresses coated in see-through plastic, then the shoes will be a microversion of that. Camden Market hippie? Then you must take a look at the patchwork boots. Butterfly-print cocktail dress? The shoes are guaranteed to match. Gangster suits? There's the perfect pair of men's lace-ups for women. A quick glance through the company's shoe archives will give an overview of every collection since their inception in 1985. An utterly mad mix of gold brocade heels, hooker-style shoes decorated with brash flowers, clashing colours and sparkly crystal pumps says it all.

FENDI

The Fendi sisters, who sold a percentage of their business to Prada in 1999, have been in business since just after the Second World War, when they joined the family company set up by their brothers in 1925. Since then, their distinctive double-F logo has become easily one of the most recognizable in fashion. Fendi's phenomenal success with the covetable baguette bag in the late 1990s

catapulted them right back into the fashion spotlight under the ever-watchful eye of design guru Karl Lagerfeld. The logo mania of 1999 and 2000 meant that Fendi became one of the most fashionable labels money could buy, whether it appears on a bag, a belt, a scarf or, of course, a pair of shoes. Associated with Fendi since the 1970s, Karl Lagerfeld acts as creative director; in 2007 the brand staged the world's first fashion show on the Great Wall of China.

FENDI SHOES ARE AS DESIRABLE AS THE LUXURY COMPANY'S HANDBAGS

FERRAGAMO

In October 1999 Ferragamo, the Italian family-run shoe and fashion house, bought a pair of shoes at Christie's in New York. The shoes belonged to Marilyn Monroe and were made for her by the Neapolitan-born Salvatore Ferragamo, who founded his company as a teenager. Before the outbreak of World War I, he designed and made shoes for the wives of dignitaries in his home village of Bonito. Ferragamo came from humble beginnings and was one of 14 children. Over the twentieth century, his shoes became legendary, helped at the beginning by his move to the US in 1914. He found a job in a shoe factory in Boston, but soon moved to be with his brothers in Santa Barbara, California, where he secured work creating cowboy boots for the American Film Company. Ferragamo began producing shoes for the silent-movie industry and became a success overnight. He was not just regarded as the shoemaker for the movies, but

SALVATORE TAKES A CELEBRITY FITTING, RIGHT. THE CLASSIC AUDREY PUMP, BELOW; STOCKING SHOES FOR AUTUMN/WINTER 2000—01, OPPOSITE LEFT

for the stars personally as well. In 1928 he returned to Florence to sort out business at home and continued work as shoemaker to the stars while expanding his business across Italy with stores from Milan to Naples. Word continued to spread about Ferragamo's genius for creating innovative shapes and using exotic materials, including python skin and gold, while guaranteeing the shoes achieved

perfection as regards comfort and fit. In addition to Gloria Swanson, Greta Garbo, Audrey Hepburn, Marilyn Monroe and Katharine Hepburn, Ferragamo also made shoes for the Duchess of Windsor and the cream of high society in Europe. They loved his fine mix of artistry and craftsmanship, and his constant stream of fresh ideas – from wedges to 'invisible' sandals held in place by invisible thread, deconstructed stilettos, odd-shaped heels, platform soles of cork or Bakelite, flat lace-ups for everyday wear, his use of raffia for sandals and intricate embroidery on evening shoes. He was truly a magician. Ferragamo died in 1960, but his wife Wanda and their children kept the business, expanding into fashion and handbags. For autumn/winter 2000–01, the house revived the classic Ferragamo wedge and the Monroe shoe has been reproduced as a special edition.

THE **FERRAGAMO** LEGACY SPANS TWO DECADES DURING WHICH THE DESIGNER BECAME SHOEMAKER TO THE STARS

FREE LANCE

French company Free Lance is also a family business. It was created by Guy and Yvon Rautureau and established by their grandfather in La Gaubretière in northern France in 1870. Over a century later, Guy and Yvon continue to produce their shoes in the same factory.

In addition to its own collections, including brands No Name, Schmoove and Pom d'Api, Free Lance has worked with designer Boudicca and Marcus Constable in London, as well as with John Galliano and Martine Sitbon in Paris. Celebrity clients have included Madonna, Cindy Crawford, Yasmin Le Bon and Kylie Minogue.

FREE LANCE SHOES ARE OUT THERE – GLAMOROUS, SEXY AND FASHIONABLE

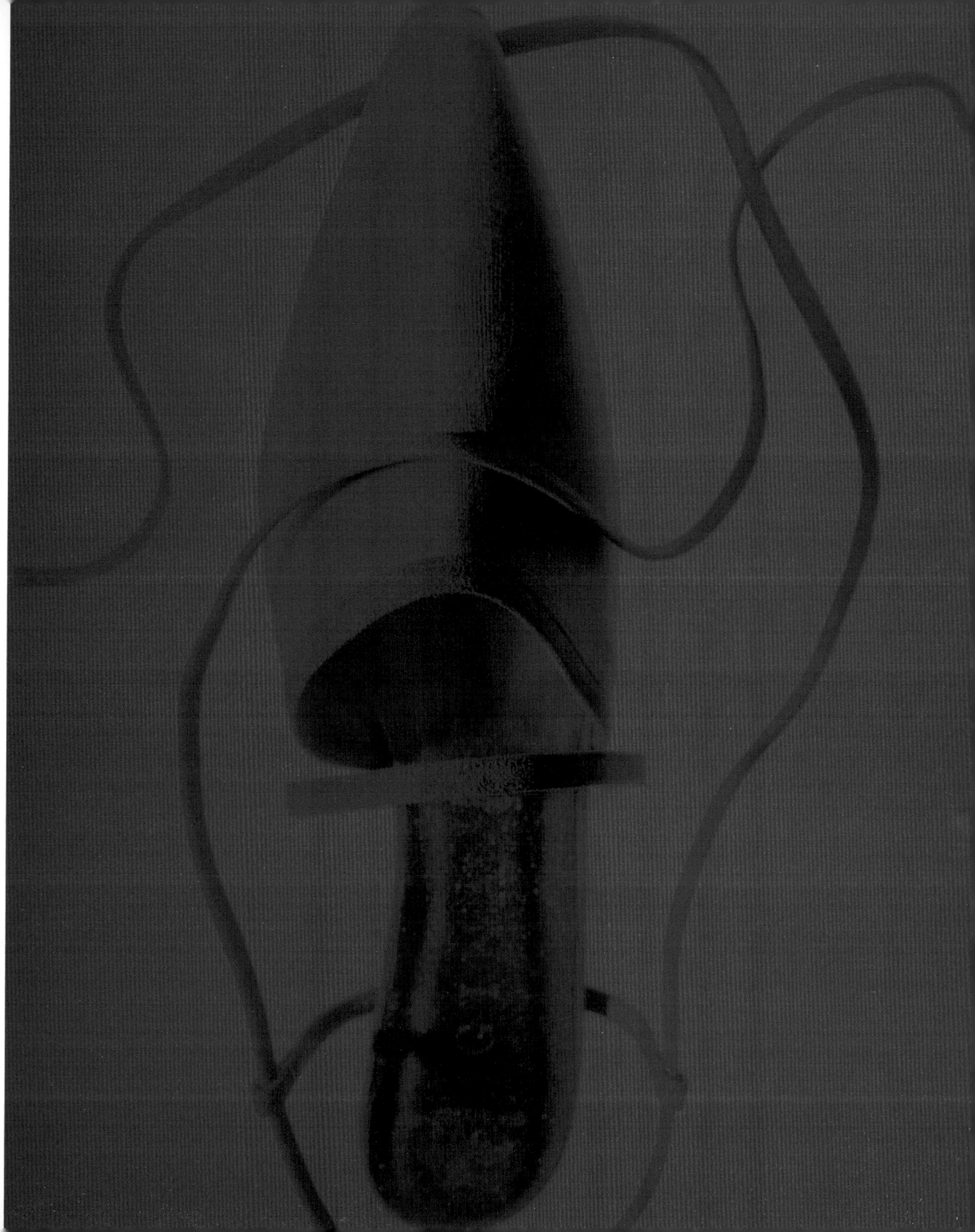

GINA

GINA SHOES ATTRACT
A GLITZY CLIENTELE,
INCLUDING MADONNA
AND MARIAH CAREY

Kate Winslet swears by hers. So, too, do Paris Hilton, Cheryl Cole, Britney Spears and Madonna, who had a pair of shoes custom-made for her 'American Pie' video, with a special slingback added so that she could dance without losing them. Madonna wore the shoes to the London Film Awards and bought a pair in every colour – gold, silver and red. Mariah Carey purchased a boot called, appropriately enough, Rockstar. As the name suggests, the boots were ultra glam and were covered in Swarovski crystals. Whitney Houston had a pair made in cashmere to match her dress. Gina, the British company established in the 1950s by Mehmet Kurdash and still run from Hackney in East London by his three sons, has become a sought-after shoe label among rock stars and showbiz celebs, who can rely on the company to produce something that will wow their audience or stun the paparazzi on the whenever they walk down the red carpet. These are luxury shoes with pizzazz. Gina is even listed in the Guinness Book of Records for producing the most expensive shoes ever made. And the price? $25,000. A few pairs were even sold, too.

GUCCI

Opened in Florence in 1922 by Guccio Gucci, the Italian family business was originally established as a saddlery specialist. Sadly, Guccio died in 1953, leaving the house in the incapable hands of his sons, who eventually managed to destroy the reputation of the brand in the fashion and accessories world. As the 1980s drew to a close, Gucci loafers became the symbol of the tacky playboy, the more-money-than-style businessman. However, in 1994 the company's new owners struck gold in the form of Texas-native designer Tom Ford, who has turned the label into one of the sleekest, most to-die-for brands in the world.

GUCCI'S SHOES ARE GUARANTEED TO MAKE FASHION VICTIMS' HEADS SPIN. THEY RANGE FROM THE REFINED – A PAIR OF ELEGANT SLINGBACKS – TO THE DOWNRIGHT SHOW OFF, WITH A PAIR OF DROP-DEAD RHINESTONE-ENCRUSTED HEELS

GUCCI'S AGGRESSIVE MARCH ON THE SHOE AND LUXURY GOODS MARKET IS EXEMPLIFIED BY THESE STEELY HEELS. YOU WOULDN'T WANT TO GET ON THE WRONG SIDE OF THEM

Ford looked back through the archives for inspiration and then reinvented the Gucci myth in the areas of fashion, fragrance and, of course, the celebrated handbags. However, it is the shoe department of the store on Milan's via

WHATEVER APPEARS ON THE GUCCI CATWALK TWICE A YEAR IS SURE TO ATTRACT RIP-OFFS ACROSS THE STREET. FOR TRUE GUCCI GALS, HOWEVER, ONLY THE REAL THING WILL DO

Montenapoleone that is raided by a plague of couture locusts twice a year during the Milan collections, when the fashion world stocks up on the coming season's slingbacks, spikes and sandals. Ford left Gucci in 2004 and the creative director is now Frida Giannini.

Gucci's waiting lists are legendary. There were the car-finish patent pumps and then there were the crocodile slingback pointies that brought fashion followers out in a cold sweat. Gucci's high-flyers have included a slinky pair of beaded, feathered slingbacks and ruched velvet boots guaranteed to make their wearer feel just like a rock star.

PIERRE HARDY

Pierre Hardy is known both for his own collection of shoes and bags as well as his role as creative director for Hermès, where he designs shoes, accessories and jewellery. He launched his first women's shoe collection for summer 1999 and opened the first Pierre Hardy boutique in the Jardins du Palais Royal in 2003. In 2010 he opened his first US flagship store in New York City's West Village.

Hardy was born in Paris. He grew up learning to dance and, after graduating with a degree in fine arts from the École Normale Supérieure, he joined a professional dance company. Multitalented, he worked as an illustrator in the mid-1980s for magazines including Italian *Vanity Fair* and started designing shoe collections for Christian Dior in 1987. He became creative director for the women's and men's shoe collections at Hermès in 1990. Since 2001 he has also worked with Nicolas Ghesquère at Balenciaga and, in 2007, collaborated with Gap to create a capsule collection of shoes available at a much lower price point.

One of the world's most influential shoe designers, his work for Balenciaga is always at the cutting edge of fashion and he constantly pushes the boundaries of shoe design, creating miniature works of art. With a strong, graphic eye, Hardy plays with proportion, shape, blocks of colour and volume in a way that consistently keeps him ahead of the pack.

RHIANNA WEARING PIERRE HARDY SHOE-BOOTS IN DECEMBER 2000, RIGHT. HARDY'S TWO-TONE BOOT, OPPOSITE TOP, WAS A SELL-OUT FOR HIGH-STREET RETAILER GAP, WHILE HIS COLOUR-BLOCK SUEDE WEDGE, BELOW, WAS TOP OF THE LINE

EMMA HOPE

She calls her shoes 'regalia for feet'. Certainly, 'shoes' seems far too mundane a word to describe Emma Hope's flights of fancy. Emma Hope Shoes was first established in 1985, shortly after the designer graduated from Cordwainers College. The following year she opened a store in Islington, north London, where she also chose to base her studio. Right from the beginning, Hope's shop was a popular destination for all footwear enthusiasts, especially those on a mission to find the perfect pair of wedding shoes. Her pastel-colored

LONDON-BASED EMMA HOPE KNOWS
HOW TO MAKE EVERYTHING FROM
A CLASSIC WEDDING SLIPPER TO A PAIR
OF FUNKY ZEBRA-PRINT LOAFER MULES

satin, brocade and silk mules are many girls' wedding-day
dream and there is a dedicated line of wedding styles. In
addition to expanding and developing her own
collection of shoes, Hope has designed for
Anna Sui, Betty Jackson, Nicole Farhi and
Paul Smith. Styles range from sparkly
ballerinas and trainers (sneakers)
to platforms and kitten heels.

CHARLES JOURDAN

The Charles Jourdan name was created in 1921, but did not become fashionable until the 1950s, when the first Parisian store opened. The company is based in the Vercors mountain range of France, where a plentiful water supply makes the perfect manufacturing base for leather goods; thanks to Charles Jourdan, it has become the manufacturing capital for luxury footwear. Each pair of shoes is treated in its own right and undergoes almost 200 different processes, from the cutting of the leather to the stitching and finishing of the upper shoe. Charles Jourdan shoes are designed for women who like an arch in their foot and a reasonable heel; women who seek glamour rather than practicality.

CHARLES JOURDAN'S SHOES ARE THE ESSENCE OF FRENCH CHIC, WITH PERFECTLY JUDGED HEELS AND FEMININE DETAILS

The shoes became cult footwear during the 1970s after the photographer Guy Bourdin produced a scandalous advertising campaign and did for Charles Jourdan what Helmut Newton had done for Yves Saint Laurent. In 1996 the firm created a perfume, called Stiletto, to honour its 75th birthday. In 2003, the Canadian shoe designer Patrick Cox was named head designer of Charles Jourdan but left in 2005 when he was replaced by Josephus Thimister.

JOURDAN'S SHOES WERE WORN BY THE STUDIO 54 GENERATION OF THE 1970S; THEY HAD BEEN INSPIRED BY THE PHOTOGRAPHER GUY BOURDIN'S SEXY ADVERTISING CAMPAIGNS

STÉPHANE KÉLIAN

Stéphane Kélian joined the Kélian family business in 1975. The French company was already 15 years old and had been set up by his two brothers, George and Gerard Kéloglanian. Up to that point, Kélian shoes had a reputation for producing luxury classic men's shoes, with a signature hand-woven leather upper. When Kélian joined the business, he increased the company profile by launching women's shoes, paying close attention to glamour and fashion. By 1978 Stéphane Kélian was established, along with the ladies' version of the woven shoe for men. By the mid-1980s Stéphane Kélian had become a famous name in both men's and women's shoes and a destination store for visitors to Paris. The design office, in Romans, has a museum next door that displays the archives.

Kélian shoes are the ultimate French shoe – never vulgar and always immaculately made. What sets the shoes apart is the variation of styles and height of heels. The brand offers women a

STÉPHANE KÉLIAN FOOTWEAR IS ALWAYS WELL-JUDGED AND IMMACULATELY MADE WITH ATTENTION PAID TO THE FINEST DETAILS, SCULPTING AN EXAGGERATED HEEL ON A BOOT, LEFT, OR CHOOSING UNUSUAL AND LUXURIOUS MATERIALS, ABOVE

HEELS ARE KÉLIAN'S SPECIALTY.
THE TINY COMMA HEEL, LEFT, HAS
ALL THE ELEGANCE OF A HEEL BUT
WITHOUT THE HEIGHT

choice, whether they are after something preppy or drop-dead sexy. A collection

might include a pair of his 'comma heel' kitten heels, an ankle-strap thong,

a rhinestone-encrusted satin stiletto or a wedge which, he insists, always

looks elegant and never chunky. The elusive combination of luxury,

comfort and style is key. His leather sandals, delicately

embroidered with sprawling handwriting in gold

thread, look as good off the foot as on it.

A SLINGBACK WEDGE,
RIGHT, IN VIVID EYE-
CATCHING COLOUR

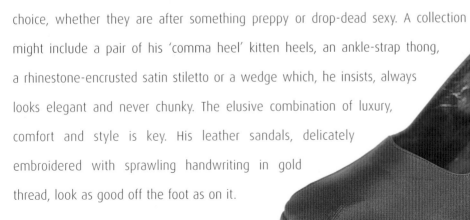

NICHOLAS KIRKWOOD

Born in Germany, Nicholas Kirkwood arrived at Central Saint Martins College of Art and Design in London at the age of 18 to do a foundation course in fine art. After a chance meeting with Philip Treacy on a skiing trip, he was offered a job at the milliner's London studio. In 2001, he began the shoemaking course at Cordwainers College in London's East End but left to return to Philip Treacy. By 2005, after creating shoes for Ghost and John Rocha, he had earned enough money to launch a solo collection. From the beginning, Kirkwood made shoes with innovative architectural shapes and the most luxurious materials. When Cecilia Dean, editor of *Visionaire* in New York, saw his collection, she introduced him to Rodarte, founded by Kate and Laura Mulleavy, and he has been making shoes for the cult label ever since. One of his signatures is a sculptural platform and a super-high heel with graphic cut-out shapes on the the leather, which give his shoes a futuristic quality.

A SHOE FROM THE KEITH HARING COLLECTION, ABOVE, WITH PRELIMINARY SKETCH, RIGHT. ANOTHER HARING VERSION APPEARS OPPOSITE TOP

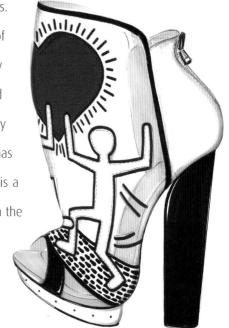

In March 2008 he became the accessories designer at Pollini and in the same year won the Swarovski Award for emerging talent for accessories at the British Fashion Awards. For spring/summer 2012, Kirkwood designed highly individual and creative shoes for Peter Pilotto (beautiful Perspex heels and woven, bejewelled plastic with a tropical island feel), Erdem (lovely painted silks), Roksanda Ilincic (block colours in an artist's palette), Meadham Kirchhoff (crazy, metallic frilled wedges) and his own label, showing just how versatile and endlessly creative he can be.

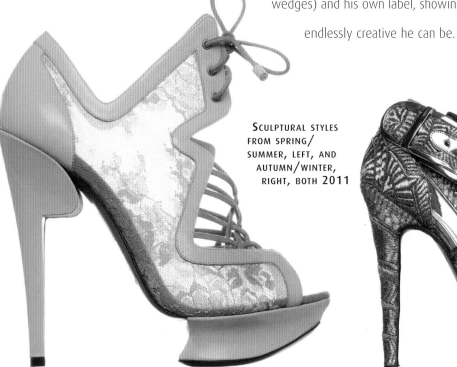

SCULPTURAL STYLES FROM SPRING/SUMMER, LEFT, AND AUTUMN/WINTER, RIGHT, BOTH **2011**

CHRISTIAN LOUBOUTIN

Christian Louboutin's shoes are very French and very feminine. Which is why women from Madison Avenue to Sloane Street love them. He started designing shoes for the stage – 'Showgirls,' he says, 'are the best to design for because they wear nothing but a pair of shoes and a feather boa.' Showgirls of another kind – Christina Aguilera, Beyoncé and Lady Gaga – have all flocked to Louboutin for their footwear needs and especially for footwear frivolities. 'Chaussures are like a jewel,' says the shoemaker, who trained with Roger Vivier. 'It's the idea of pure luxury. If you offer a woman a beautiful ring, the magical moment is when she opens the box, Voila! I have to show my shoes in the same way.' When the French film star Arielle Dombasle had a pair of shoes made for her by Louboutin, they came with a love letter from her husband locked into a see-through heel, along with a lock of his hair and a quill – the ultimate love token. Louboutin's shoes mix fantasy and art with romance, fashion and craft. They are instantly recognizable from their bright red soles. As Louboutin himself says, 'I like women to see my shoes as objects of beauty, as gems outside their own universe. Shoes are not an accessory; they're an attribute.'

LOUBOUTIN'S SHOES ARE SEXY, COQUETTISH AND VERY SHOWY. THE SOLES OF HIS SHOES, OPPOSITE, ARE ALWAYS A DISTINCTIVE RED

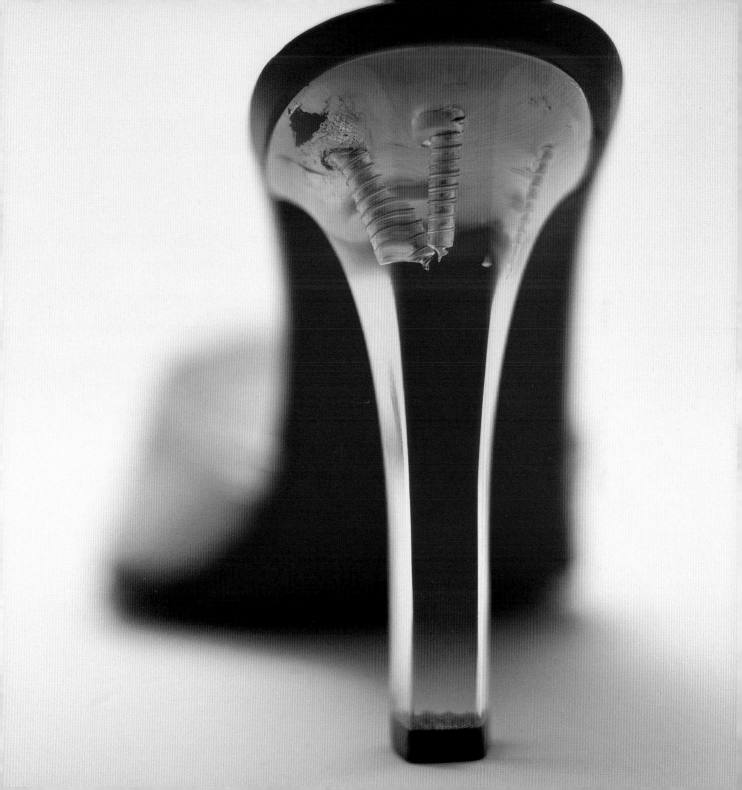

Credited with bringing the stiletto back into fashion in the late 1990s and 2000s, Louboutin is known for some of the highest heels in the business, with dozens of styles featuring heel heights of 13 cm (5 inches) or more and platforms of 2.5–5 cm (1–2 inches). Beloved of actresses and celebrities, who often are seen wearing the red-soled shoes on the red carpet, Louboutin is quite possibly the most highly recognized footwear brand in the world. Christian, who began his career freelancing for Maud Frizon, Chanel and Yves Saint Laurent, and then went on to work with such fashion houses as Lanvin, Chloé, Givenchy and Jean Paul Gaultier, has recently created shoes for Rodarte and Roland Mouret.

CLOCKWISE FROM RIGHT, PARISIAN STYLE
FROM LOUBOUTIN: RED SILK PUMPS,
SILVER CRYSTAL PEEP-TOES, GREEN SUEDE
GRESSIMO ANKLE-STRAPS AND LACE-UP
SNAKESKIN SANDALS

STELLA McCARTNEY

Stella McCartney graduated from Central St Martins in London in 1995 and in 1997 she was appointed creative director of Chloé in Paris. In 2001, she launched her own fashion house with the Gucci Group, which is now the PPR Luxury Group. Since then, she has won numerous awards and was also included in *Time* magazine's 100 most influential people for 2009. In September 2010, McCartney was appointed creative director for the 2012 Olympics by Adidas, in order to make the official outfits for the the British team. McCartney's easy, sporty daywear and feminine eveningwear scored her many fans, from Madonna and Gwyneth Paltrow to 'real' women who simply rely on her clothes for everyday life – such as the school

run or entertaining after work. McCartney, a working mother of four, understands what makes women tick and how clothes can help them in their daily lives. She has also become a bit of a genius at coming up with accessories – particularly bags and shoes – that are both wearable and cool. However, what sets her apart in the luxury goods market is her strict vegetarianism that underpins everything she does.

In 2009 she launched Meat-Free Mondays with her father, Paul, to encourage people to eat less meat and she practises what she preaches. She doesn't use fur or leather in any of her designs, but as far as her shoes and bags are concerned, you would never know. The faux leather looks like the real thing and she makes use of innovative and eco-friendly materials, such as woven raffia, to great effect. Whether you are vegetarian or not, the shoes have the same appeal.

ETHICAL AND ELEGANT: BLACK AND NUDE FAUX PATENT ANKLE-STRAP MORGANA STILETTO, ABOVE; A FAUX NAPPA LEATHER ROUND-TOE DUMAS PUMP WITH CHOKED THROAT, LEFT, AND NUDE MESH BASKET SANDALS, OPPOSITE

ALEXANDER McQUEEN

By the time of his tragic death in 2010, Alexander McQueen's extraordinary 30 cm (12 inch) armadillo heels were in the shops and on the feet of celebrities everywhere including, of course, Lady Gaga, who wore them for her 'Bad Romance' video. In patterned snakeskin, they looked like some sort of primeval reptilian prosthetic. While the models in the show for McQueen's remarkable Atlantis collection walked perfectly (the shoes have a chunky platform inside), they are about statement and attitude, not comfort.

McQueen launched his label in 1992 and his clothes – and the shoes that were designed to be worn with them – were always provocative and controversial. Despite his untimely death, 2011 was an important year for the Alexander McQueen brand, which has continued to operate under the leadership of McQueen's right-hand woman, Sarah Burton. She scored a double whammy with both a major retrospective at the Metropolitan Museum in New York in 2011

CORSETRY DETAILING IN MCQUEEN'S AUTUMN/WINTER 2011 LACE-UP BOOTS GIVES A VICTORIAN GOTH FEEL, WHILE HIS REPTILIAN AND ARMADILLA SHOES, OPPOSITE, ARE FROM 2010

and the Royal Wedding where Burton's dress for Catherine Middleton was kept a closely guarded secret until the moment she stepped out in front of the cameras. The dress – and, of course, the matching handmade shoes – were later displayed at Buckingham Palace. The shoes themselves looked as though they had barely touched the ground with their immaculate handmade lace, which matched the dress, painstakingly created by the Royal School of Needlework at Hampton Court.

For mere mortals however, it is still possible to live a fantasy life in a pair of Alexander McQueen shoes – most likely with platforms, buckles, skull details or a sexy peep-toe. Rest assured, they will be more suitable for a warrior princess than the future Queen of England.

RODOLPHE MÉNUDIER

Born in 1961, the French shoe maestro Rodolphe Ménudier cannot remember a time when he did not feel passionate about shoes. Consequently, like many fashion designers, there was only one path his career could take. Ménudier has perfected both the art and the craft of the shoe. With his spindly, fragile heels, spiky metal stilettos, futuristic moulded curves of Perspex and daring colour palette, he is one of those designers who can make a girl melt. Aficionados love him. His shoes are sold in department stores, as well as in some of the hippest boutiques.

His first job after leaving college in 1986 was as house designer with Michel Perry. There, he developed the art of making a couture shoe, learnt business skills and forged valuable contacts with couturiers with whom he has also worked – Paco Rabanne, Karl Lagerfeld (at both Chanel and Chloé), Balenciaga, Christian Lacroix (whose shoes were always high, elegant and made in sumptuous shades of satin) and Christian Dior.

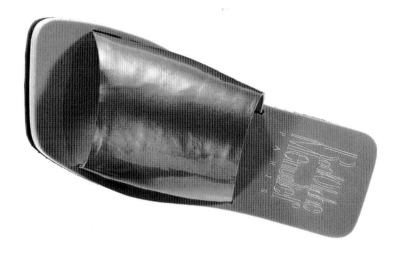

RODOLPHE MÉNUDIER
IS A FASHION-EDITOR
FAVOURITE. THE FRENCH
DESIGNER'S RISQUÉ,
SEXY SHOES HAVE A
SENSE OF ADVENTURE,
BE IT AN ELEGANT
SLIPPER OR A DISCO
DAZZLER WITH A
PERSPEX SOLE AND
GOLD STRAPS

Every one of Ménudier's shoes is perfect, with the most beautiful balance of colour, height and detail, as befits the precise world of haute couture. With just six styles, he launched his own collection in 1994, which he dubbed 'haute couture high tech'. His trademarks are innovation and a creative use of colour and materials, as reflected in his sexy, zipped boots; in other words, footwear that gets a girl noticed. The shoes pictured here demonstrate his flexibility as a designer as well as his innate modernity. A beaded mule is finished with a clear Perspex heel like a block of ice, while a gold strappy sandal is given an innovative sole made from a single piece of Perspex, moulded both to support and show off the foot.

The Ménudier headquarters are close to the Place des Victoires, in the second arrondissement in Paris. In the autumn of 2000 he opened his first stand-alone store – two whole floors of Rodolphe Ménudier – in one of the city's chicest shopping areas. For many women, it was almost like entering the gates of heaven.

CHARLOTTE OLYMPIA

Charlotte Olympia Dellal is fashion royalty. Her Brazilian mother, Andrea, was a model and her sister, Alice, is currently a model. Her brother, Alex, runs an art gallery. As a child, Charlotte remembers trying on her mother's shoes – they made a profound impression – and she now makes some of the most glamorous and fabulous footwear on the market, both under her own label and in collaboration with other designers, including Clements Ribeiro, Peter Som and Alice Temperley.

Dellal graduated from the London shoe school, Cordwainers, in 2004 and worked at Ungaro and Giambattista Valli before launching her own label in 2007. Her shoes are all handcrafted in Italy and have a trademark gold spider's web on the sole. She has a flagship store in London's Mayfair and sells to some of the world's most discerning shoe lovers, including Sarah Jessica Parker, Kate Moss, Keira Knightley, Katy Perry and Beyoncé.

Dellal mixes up classic shapes with retro 1940s glamour. There might be a suede lace-up wedge in gold and black stripes, a leopard-print court perched on top of a shiny lacquer red platform, or a classic black suede court with a dramatic gold platform sculpted beneath it. Her spring/summer 2012 collection had a 1950s Miami beach

theme, with mermaid models showing off shoes in Art Deco pastels, deckchair stripes and pink flamingo feathers. Charlotte is her own best advert – her shoes always look immaculate with their cool retro glamour and are feminine and elegant, usually with a witty twist.

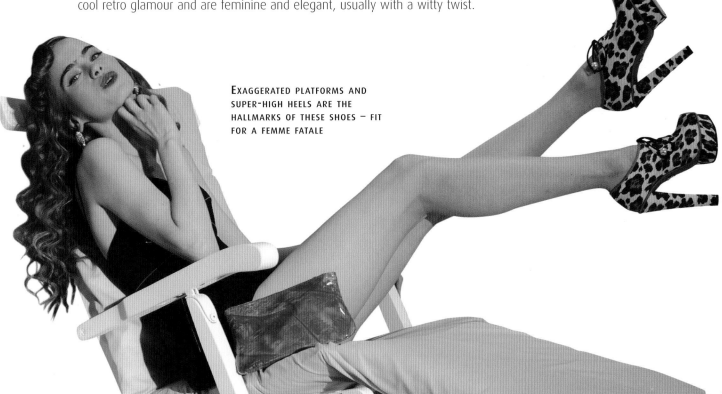

EXAGGERATED PLATFORMS AND SUPER-HIGH HEELS ARE THE HALLMARKS OF THESE SHOES – FIT FOR A FEMME FATALE

THERE IS SOMETHING ABOUT
THE SNUG FIT AND ELONGATED
CHISELLED TOES OF MICHEL
PERRY'S BOOTS, COWBOY OR
OTHERWISE, THAT MAKES
THEM VERY SEDUCTIVE

MICHEL **PERRY**

On the rue St Honoré in Paris, Michel Perry's shop is the essence of everything that is French.

The shop is all curlicues, delicate pinks and pastel shades. It's as French as a madame's boudoir.

In addition to shoes, there are clothes, hand-picked from various designers. But the women who make

a pilgrimage to the shop each season – both at the beginning and at the end when the sale starts –

are interested in only one thing: their feet.

Perry, who trained at the École des Beaux-Arts in the centre of Paris, has been producing shoes, boots

and delicate slippers since 1987. He can make a sensible Mary Jane like no one else can, giving it his own

special spin, with an accentuated arch to the foot and a heel so well defined that it offers both height and

perfect balance. One season he painted a design onto the leather heel of one of his elongated shoes.

Another time, he let the supple kid leather speak for itself, leaving it completely plain, with just the tiniest of buckles fastening the shoe to the foot. The secret of his shoes – and what makes women come back for more, time and again – is the long, pointy shapes that he has perfected, which make the feet look impossibly slender and feminine. There is something very sensual about having your foot zipped into a Michel Perry boot. It's enough to make a woman hand over her credit card without so much as checking the price.

Not only does he sell his own collection in exclusive stores around the world, Perry has also collaborated with several fashion designers on designs for their own lines. Kostas Murkudis, Jean Colonna and the avant-garde talent Gaspard Yurkievich have all used his finely tuned eye to create exquisite footwear to complement their fashion fantasies.

PRADA

Just one red stripe is all it took and the dedicated followers of fashion were at Miuccia Prada's feet. Literally. Prada, the family company founded in 1913 by Miuccia's grandfather Mario as a business making trunks and suitcases to order for wealthy Italians, has become the leader of all trends in shoes. What Miuccia puts on the catwalk in spring will be copied in the chains by summer and stripped from the shelves as soon as stock arrives in Prada boutiques around the world. The great Prada renaissance was brought about by a

simple black nylon bag with a black-and-gold triangular logo. But it has been sustained by a clever strategy: seducing women at their most vulnerable point – their feet. Every season, the fashion pack take their seats at the Prada show in the tiny Milan catwalk theatre and wait with bated breath. It's not so much the clothes they want to see, but the shoes. They are even highlighted on an easy-to-view video screen so that anyone in the back rows can get a closer look.

PRADA'S COLLECTION FOR
SPRING/SUMMER 2000 WAS
A VINTAGE ONE, WITH
GLOSSY PATENT-LEATHER
HEELS WITH CUT-OUTS AND
KITTEN-HEEL SLINGBACKS

And although they might be working, putting together trends, news stories and ideas for shoots for the season ahead, they cannot resist making a mental shopping list. Because it's guaranteed there will be a shoe here that will keep them awake at night; they will not be able to rest until they are wearing it. From the Prada main line, there have been bestsellers, like the Mary Janes with appliquéd leather leaves sprouting all over them, 1930s silver-screen-goddess shoes with chunky gold heels and Art Deco styling, sweet little mules with a bow at the front and a kitten heel, red-and-white patent-leather 1960s-inspired Mod shoes and sporty trainer-style slip-ons in iridescent blue or

pink. Every shoe is a statement. And Miuccia knows how to strike just the right chord. Then there is Miu Miu, the more accessible younger sister line to Prada, featuring cowhide mules and shoes with moulded heels, neoprene uppers and fluorescent heels. And most recently, Prada Sport has been launched, the collection of aerodynamic trainers, sporty (rather than sports) shoes and toggle boots that has made a simple red stripe into the ultimate status symbol. In fashion, they are all, quite simply, 'to die for.'

SPORTS INFLUENCES ARE EVIDENT IN THIS HYBRID TRAINER BOOT, FAR LEFT, WHILE STRAPPY LEATHER AND SUEDE SANDALS ARE GIVEN A MODERN EDGE WITH A STRIPE OF SPORTY ELASTIC ON THE SLINGBACK, FAR LEFT, TOP; CHEQUERBOARD PLATFORMS, LEFT, ARE FROM 2011 AND SLINGBACKS WITH A 1950s CADILLAC-ERA DESIGN, TOP, ARE FROM 2012

RED **OR DEAD**

Wayne and Gerardine Hemingway are the founders of Red or Dead, the company that began life in 1982 as a stall in Camden Market, selling secondhand clothing and footwear. They were hugely influential in the 1980s, both for their own shoe designs and for their idea to introduce Dr Martens work boots as part of their stock. Jean-Paul Gaultier bought them from the Red or Dead market stall, and they became an icon of the 1980s, worn by everyone from Sade to Demi Moore.

Disco glitter mules reflect Red or Dead's goodtime attitude

Red or Dead's own designs hit the spot, too; from the 1987 Watch Shoe – a chunky, ripple-soled lace-up that fastened with a wristwatch as a buckle – which sold out after boy band Bros took to wearing them wherever they went, to the 1990 Space Baby collection featuring a picture of a baby's head in an astronaut's helmet,

stitched into transparent Dr Martens boots. Red or Dead's shoes were largely unisex, offering a totally different style of footwear than was available in chain stores at midmarket prices. They were the shoes of the arty individual, always a little left-field, and guaranteed to bring a good dose of wit and humour to their customers' feet.

In the 1990s the company continued to take a sideways view of footwear, while expanding its fashion collections, too, with themes ranging from Indian Summer to Geography Teacher and New York Dolls. Today, the business includes wristwatches, glasses and handbags in addition to footwear.

RED OR DEAD HAVE AN IRREVERENT APPROACH TO FOOTWEAR

REPETTO

In 1947, Rose Repetto made her first pair of ballet slippers – designed for her own son, the dancer and choreographer Roland Petit, to dance in. Soon the world's best ballerinas were wearing the slippers, including Rudolf Nureyev and Kirov. Word spread and by 1956, when Repetto made the now infamous handcrafted Cendrillon ballerina for Brigitte Bardot to wear in ...*And God Created Woman*, a footwear legend was born. Repetto opened her first shop in Paris in 1959, selling artisan-made shoes and pumps. Today, the store is still at 22 rue de la Paix, near the Opera Garnier in Paris.

Repetto, who bought the British ballet shoe company Gamba in 1992, continue to make ballet shoes, not least for the Opera National de Paris, but are now probably better known for their ballerina pumps worn by everyone from Catherine Deneuve to Sofia Coppola and Hillary Clinton. The company has collaborated with avant-garde labels Issey Miyake and Yohji Yamamoto, as well as Comme des Garçons, who made over the ballerina and also the lace-up

Zizi pump (a favourite of Serge Gainsbourg and Mick Jagger, no less) to give an extra fashion edge. In 2005, Repetto sold its one millionth ballerina.

Repetto offers a service where customers can choose from an almost endless choice of colours and leathers to create their own ballerina, made to personal specifications, enabling them to choose leather and trim in any preferred combination. It's not surprising that in the bag of every high-heel wearer, there lurks a pair of flats – and if you are lucky, they will be Repetto ballerinas.

A FAVOURITE OF BRIGITTE BARDOT, THE REPETTO BALLERINA NEVER GOES OUT OF STYLE

S E R G I O **R O S S I**

It's no wonder that Gucci chose to buy a 70 per cent stake in Sergio Rossi in November 1999. In the world's most fashionable circles, Rossi's super-sexy high heels were giving Gucci's own designs a run for their money. (Not literally, of course; these shoes are not intended to be worn for running anywhere.) At the time, you could glance along the front row of any fashion show in Milan and there would be as many Rossis as Guccis and Pradas dangling elegantly from the feet of the fashion cognoscenti. Located on Milan's chic via Montenapoleone, the store would be constantly packed with fashionistas competing for the highest, strappiest heels. These are shoes designed for making an entrance; the more flirtatious and brighter, the better. Risky heels for risqué women. Shoes that spell sex.

Only a man could be responsible for such high-voltage footwear and when Rossi first began designing shoes as a young boy in San Mauro Pascoli in the 1950s, he should really have been questioned as to the purity of his thoughts. His father had crafted made-to-measure shoes before him and that was

SERGIO ROSSI'S
LEAF SHOE, LEFT, FROM
HIS COLLECTION FOR
SPRING/SUMMER 2000

where Rossi began his apprenticeship. During the 1970s, his shoes were talked about by women who liked to party. By the 1980s, Rossi was producing shoes for Gianni Versace, Dolce & Gabbana and Azzedine Alaïa. Rossi shoes were the perfect complement to a curvy Versace couture gown or a stretchy little Alaïa number. While the designer knew how to make women – and their male friends – salivate over his shoes, he also possessed a good degree of business acumen and began to open his own stores. Outlets in Milan, Florence and Rome were followed by others across Europe, as well as in New York and the Far East. In 2008 Francesco Russo was appointed creative director of the brand with his first collection debuting for autumn/winter 2009.

FAERIES, CARNIVALS AND MAGICAL WORLDS DOMINATE THE AUTUMN/WINTER **2011** COLLECTION. CLOCKWISE FROM ABOVE: SATURNIA, ARLECCHINO AND TORTUOSA

SUPERMODELS LOVE ROSSI'S ELABORATE BOOTS AND STRAPPY HEELS, LIKE THE METALLIC ONES OPPOSITE

RUPERT SANDERSON

Rupert Sanderson names every pair of shoes he makes after a daffodil – already there are over 26,000 registered so he will never run out of inspiration. Sanderson is a minimalist – his shoes are perfectly honed, the perfect balance of form, function and a flourish of sensuality that keeps women coming back for more. One of the few designers who seem to have perfected the art of the flat shoe, making them just as fine and elegant as his vertiginous heels, he is not driven by fashion or trends per se, but more the pursuit of shoe perfection itself. His footwear is about the line and the curve and also the softness and suppleness of the leather.

Sanderson started his career in advertising, but retrained as a shoe designer after enrolling in the two-year course in shoemaking at Cordwainers College in London. After a fact-finding mission to Italy, when he visited shoe factories and tanneries in the country, he found work at two great Italian shoe companies – Sergio Rossi and Bruno Magli – both while they were still family-run before being bought by larger luxury goods companies. During that time, he made invaluable contacts within the Italian shoemaking

TRIBAL RESORT FASHION IN THE NISSA, A MIXTURE OF TEXTURE AND COLOUR, WITH A FUCHSIA STRAP AND CORK PLATFORM WEDGE

fraternity, which stood him in good stead when he launched his own company in 2001. Five years later, he cleverly bought a controlling share in the Italian shoe factory with whom he had been working with when he started out.

Sanderson has two stores in Mayfair and Knightsbridge in London, as well as one in Hong Kong and another in Paris in the Palais Royal. Awarded the British Fashion Council's accessory designer of the year in 2008, he founded Fashion Fringe Shoes in the same year to give young designers, as he once was, a chance to show their shoes and develop their businesses. He has written a daily blog for Vogue.co.uk, where readers could follow his adventures, from meetings with Kristin Scott Thomas to roller discos and pictures from the front row at Osman Yousefzada's show, for whom Sanderson made the shoes for his spring/summer 2012 collection.

THE SUPER-HIGH HYDRA, ABOVE, IS A COLOUR-BLOCK, PATENT LEATHER PEEP-TOE, WHILE THE LOW-HEEL CLIPPER, RIGHT, IS A NUDE SLINGBACK WITH BLACK LEATHER BOW AND CUT-OUT UPPERS

SIGERSON MORRISON

Karl Sigerson grew up in Nebraska, while Miranda Morrison grew up in England. They met while studying at the Fashion Institute of Technology in New York and started their footwear line in 1991, with the mantra 'style over fashion'. It is unusual for women to design shoes – this is largely a man's world – and perhaps because of that, their footwear has always had a wearable edge: chic, confident, comfortable and cool rather than simply sexy for the sake of it. They understand that there are women who like to wear flats by day and heels by night, testing out their own designs by wearing them every day.

BOLD BLOCK COLOUR IN THE
PICASSO SANDAL, LEFT, WHILE
THE TWO-TONE WALTON, ABOVE,
IS CLASSIC NEW YORK

Their signature suede pumps and monochrome boots were handcrafted in Italy to fit beautifully as well as to flatter the leg and foot. But 20 years after founding their own label, the two designers acrimoniously parted company in 2011 (they had sold their brand to Marc Fisher in 2006 but remained as creative directors). They have been replaced by a design team who will continue to produce – and expand – the successful sister brand, Belle by Sigerson Morrison, with its chunky, wooden-heeled, Eskimo-inspired clogs, cool leather boots, high-heeled loafers, high-heeled moccasins and easy-to-wear flats. Even without Sigerson and Morrison in command, their spirit lives on and these are still shoes for cool city girls to hang out in, by day and by night.

ELEGANT LINES FOR CITY GIRLS: THE PICASSO, LEFT, AND THE PHEBE, RIGHT

TABITHA SIMMONS

The British stylist, Tabitha Simmons, has made a name for herself as the creative fashion editor behind some of the more quirky, spirited fashion stories in magazines including US *Vogue* (where she sometimes collaborates with her husband, the photographer Craig McDean), *Vogue* China, Italian *Vogue*, *Dazed & Confused* and *AnOther Magazine*, as well as *V*. Simmons, who studied film at Kingston University in the UK before becoming a fashion stylist, has also worked with Dolce & Gabbana, Chloé, Zac Posen and Balenciaga, so she knows what works in a fashion photograph and on the catwalk as well as what women want to wear on their feet. While continuing work as a stylist, she launched her shoe collection in 2009 – each pair handmade in Italy. These shoes are not just photogenic: Simmons has a devoted following and not just among her fellow fashion editors. Sienna Miller, Keira Knightley, Kate Moss,

STRIPED DUSTY STYLE IN LINEN SILK, ABOVE, AND A SUEDE PLATFORM SALLY BOOT, RIGHT; OPPOSITE, THE LACE-UP CANDACE IN VELVET

Catherine, Duchess of Cambridge, Alison Mosshart and Julianne Moore are all fans. Simmons' shoes are intricate in their detail, often incorporating interesting pattern and texture, with multilayered platforms in contrasting colours and fabrics, double ankle straps, buckles, zips and demure bows, laces, peep-toes and other design features that make her creations stand out in the crowd. Like her styling, her shoes have a story to tell – quirky but always cool.

CAMILLA SKOVGAARD

Camilla Skovgaard's designs are not for the faint-hearted. She makes shoes for smart, powerful urban girls who like to make an entrance. Since graduating from the Royal College of Art in London in 2006, the Danish-born designer has made quite an impact with her jagged-edged platforms with serrated soles and lots of zips, buckles and hardware.

Skovgaard began her career at the highest end of couture at the age of 20, when she was employed by a French fashion house in Dubai to work on the wardrobes of the world's richest women. At the age of 27, she moved to London to study shoemaking at Cordwainers College and there she developed her own label while gaining a

OFFERINGS FROM THE **2011** COLLECTIONS INCLUDE THIS CROSS-STRAP SOCK SHOE-BOOT, RIGHT, AND CUT-OUT LEATHER PLATFORM AND SAW-TOOTH ANKLE BOOT, BOTH OPPOSITE

Master's at the Royal College of Art. Her first order came from Saks Fifth Avenue in the US, who bought her graduation collection.

Despite the edgy designs of her shoes, they are also beautifully crafted and designed, fluid yet fierce. The winner of the Queen Elizabeth Scholar Award for excellence in British craftsmanship in 2007 and the accessories designer of the year award at ELLE Style Awards in 2010, her talent was recognized back home in Denmark when she also won the award for accessories designer of the year at the Dansk Fashion Awards of 2011. Her shoes are a favourite among celebrities, including Halle Berry, Rhianna and Kristen Stewart, and she sells around the globe, from Hong Kong to Dubai.

TOD'S

Tod's are the off-duty shoes of the jet set. Italian entrepreneur Diego della Valle first saw a gap in the market in the early 1980s and, having stumbled across an intriguing vintage driving shoe, he sent it to his father's shoe factory near Ancona and asked for it to be replicated. The design was a classic, but its marketing was pure genius. Almost 20 years later, Tod's is a major player in the Italian – indeed the international – luxury leather business. And like the running shoe, the driving shoe (with the knobbly heel grip in rubber) is worn for everything but driving. 'Tod's' are the Sloane's and Preppy's shoe of choice, but they are also sported by the Italian businesswoman on her travels, as well as the American fashion

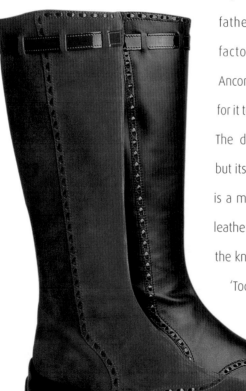

TOD'S ARE THE OFF-DUTY SHOES OF
THE JET SET – COMFORTABLE,
PRACTICAL AND CHIC

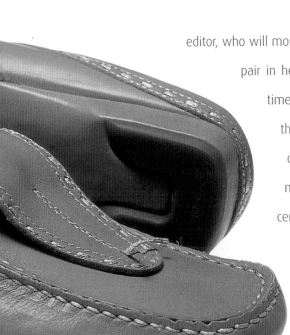

editor, who will most likely carry a pair in her bag at all times, for when the Manolos or Louboutins become too much to cope with. Tod's is a company with a century of family shoemaking behind it and this is now combined with a design and marketing expertise that keeps the brand both forward-looking and in demand. Both Gwyneth Paltrow and Anne Hathaway have been the 'faces' of the brand.

THE KNOBBLY SHOES AND HEELS OF TOD'S DRIVING SHOES HAVE BECOME A HIGHLY DESIRABLE TRADEMARK

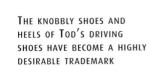

U G G

When the weather turns cold, the Ugg boots come out in droves. In the 1970s, the sheepskin-lined suede boots were worn by surfers in Australia, but Uggs – the tracksuits of the footwear world – have become the guilty pleasure of even the most fashionable. Hollywood stars wear them to keep their feet warm while filming on

location; indeed, there is a memorable picture of Sarah Jessica Parker filming *Sex and the City* in New York wearing a wedding dress with a pair of Uggs underneath. Market stallholders wear them for the same reason, though with not quite so glamorous results. When Oprah Winfrey introduced her 7 million viewers to the joys of the Ugg in 2000, the comfy, cosy, slouchy boots – and their numerous copies – became an everyday staple across America and the rest of the world followed.

The Ugg Classic short boot, which is suede lined in sheepskin, is the bestseller. Once worn, you will never want to take them off. The company has also expanded into other accessories, gloves, slippers and scarves. And for summer, there are sandals and flip-flops without a shred of fleece in sight.

The brand, which is now owned by the American company Deckers, launched a new collection of more structured shoes for autumn/winter 2011, with boots and shoes made in Italy, hand-finished in the highest-quality leather and materials. This luxury collection included a thigh-high suede boot.

ANIMAL-PRINT UGGS, OPPOSITE; RIGHT, A 2006 ADVERTISEMENT RECALLS THE SURFER ROOTS OF THE BRAND'S AUSTRALIAN ORIGINS

ROGER VIVIER

The man credited with inventing the stiletto heel in 1954 – the shoe that so perfectly accentuated Christian Dior's revolutionary designs of that decade – was, not surprisingly, known as the Heel King. He designed Queen Elizabeth's shoes for the coronation of 1953. Only he could make the shoe look so regal, and so sexy, while making it comfortable and practical at the same time. The shoes featured a special double sole that gave the Queen – a European size 37 – extra height without having to battle with a ridiculous heel. Vivier's shoes were the stuff of dreams. He preferred to call his creations *souliers* – more refined than the everyday *chaussures* – and, indeed, they were certainly anything but everyday. Roger Vivier was the couturier of the woman's foot; he was its

VIVIER'S SQUARE-BUCKLE SHOES FOR YVES SAINT LAURENT, OPPOSITE LEFT, WERE WORN BY CATHERINE DENEUVE IN *BELLE DE JOUR*. CLASSIC VIVIER CUTAWAY SHOES, OPPOSITE RIGHT. VIVIER'S RELATIONSHIP WITH YSL WAS LONG AND FRUITFUL, LEFT. PERFECT BALANCE OF SHAPE, STYLE AND FUNCTION, RIGHT

milliner, its furrier and its jeweller. He managed to create a shoe that was at once dress and coat and hairstyle and jewellery.

Born in Paris in 1907, Vivier began his apprenticeship as a bootmaker. He opened his first shop in Paris in 1937 in the ritzy rue Royale. During the war he set up shop in New York, until rations resulted in a ban on the making of new shoes. He reinvented himself as a milliner, but returned to his beloved shoes – and Paris – in time to work with Christian Dior on his New Look. In 1953 he began making shoes for Dior, and for the first time his shoes became relatively affordable and accessible to a wider audience. After Dior's death in 1957, Vivier designed for Yves Saint Laurent. Among his many innovations, he was the first to use see-through plastic and his square buckle has become the signature feature for the brand. He continued working and innovating until his death at the age of 90 in 1998.

VIVIENNE WESTWOOD

She has always had a thing about shoes: from her swashbuckling pirates and buffalo girls of the early 1980s to her rocking-horse shoes and gravity-defying platforms of the late 1990s, Vivienne Westwood's designs have always been extraordinary. For autumn/ winter 1981—82, there were pirate boots, all baggy around the ankles. In spring/ summer 1985, Westwood fans were treated to platform shoes, designed to be worn with the 'mini crini'. By the following season, her shoes had become even more outrageous. Westwood called them 'rocking-horse shoes'. And they certainly rocked. Banana-shaped wooden platforms were tied to the leg, making running for a bus pretty impossible, although Westwood herself was spotted riding her bike in them. Others, including Westwood's friend and one-time assistant Jibby Beane, didn't set foot outside in anything else;

VIVIENNE WESTWOOD'S UNIQUE SHOES ARE ALWAYS EXTREME, WHETHER IN HEIGHT, STYLE OR SUBJECT MATTER

Japanese Westwood fanatics have long since mastered the art of walking in Westwood platforms. By autumn/winter 1990–91, the shoes had grown in proportion to the Elevator platform, which, some three collections later, had reached a dizzying 25 cm (10 inches) in height. And then fashion history was made: Naomi Campbell fell off her platforms mid-sashay down the catwalk. Photographers snapped and the audience clapped as the supermodel collapsed to the floor, smiled sweetly and picked herself up like some graceful ballerina in *Swan Lake*. It was a sensation and newspapers worldwide lapped it up. The electric-blue snakeskin shoes took pride of place at London's Victoria & Albert Museum on their own pedestal.

WHEN NAOMI CAMPBELL FELL OFF HER ELEVATOR PLATFORMS, SHE MADE NEWSPAPER HEADLINES

ADDRESS BOOK

Brian Atwood
www.brianatwood.com

Birkenstock
70 Neal Street
London WC2H 9PA
Telephone: 0207 240 2783
www.birkenstock.co.uk

Manolo Blahnik
49–51 Old Church Street
London SW3 5BS
Telephone: 0207 352 3863
www.manoloblahnik.com

Camper
28 Old Bond Street
London W1X 3AB
Telephone: 0207 409 3114
www.camper.com

Chanel
19–21 Old Bond Street
London W1X 3DA
Telephone: 0207 493 3836
www.chanel.com

Jimmy Choo Couture
27 New Bond Street
London W1S 2RH
Telephone: 0207 493 5858
www.jimmychoo.com
eu.jimmychoo.com

Clarks
260 Oxford Street
London W1C 1DN
Telephone: 0207 499 0305
www.clarks.com

Dr Martens Store
17 Neal Street
Covent Garden
London WC2H 9PU
Telephone: 0207 240 7555
www.drmartens.com

Dr Scholl
www.drschollsshoes.com

Dolce & Gabbana
6–8 Old Bond Street
London W1X 3TA
Telephone: 0207 659 5300
www.dolcegabbana.com

Fendi
20–22 Sloane Street
London SW1X 9NE
Telephone: 0207 838 6288
www.fendi.com

Ferragamo
207 Sloane Street
London SW1X 9QX
Telephone: 0207 838 7730
www.ferragamo.com

Free Lance
www.sarenza.co.uk/free-lance

Gina
9 Old Bond Street
London W1X 3TA
Telephone: 0207 409 7090
www.gina.com

Gucci
34 Old Bond Street
London W1X 4HH
Telephone: 0207 629 2716
www.gucci.com

Pierre Hardy
30 Jane Street
New York
New York 10014
USA
www.pierrehardy.com

Emma Hope
53 Sloane Square
London SW1X 8AX
Telephone: 0207 259 9566
www.emmahope.com

Charles Jourdan
www.charles-jourdan.com

Stéphane Kélian
www.stephane-kelian.com

Nicholas Kirkwood
5 Mount Street
London W1K 3NE
Telephone: 0207 290 1404
www.nicholaskirkwood.com

Christian Louboutin
23 Motcomb Street
London SW1X 8LB
Telephone: 0207 245 6510
www.christianlouboutin.com

Stella McCartney
30 Bruton Street
London W1J 6QR
Telephone: 0207 518 3100
www.stellamccartney.co.uk

Alexander McQueen
4–5 Old Bond Street
London W1S 4PD
Telephone: 0207 355 0088
www.alexandermcqueen.com

Benoit Méléard
www.benoitmeleard.fr

Rodolphe Ménudier
www.rodolphemenudier.com

Charlotte Olympia
56 Maddox Street
London W1S 1AY
Telephone: 0207 499 0145
www.charlotteolympia.com

Michel Perry
www.michelperry.com

Prada
16 Old Bond Street
London W1S 4PS
Telephone: 0207 647 5000
www.prada.com

Red or Dead
Pentland Centre
Lakeside, Squires Lane
London N3 2QL
Telephone: 0208 457 5005
www.redordead.com

Repetto
www.repetto.com

Rupert Sanderson
19 Bruton Place
London W1J 6LZ
Telephone: 0207 491 2220
www.rupertsanderson.com

Sergio Rossi
12a Beauchamp Place
Knightsbridge
London SW3 1NQ
Telephone: 0207 225 0663
www.sergiorossi.com

Sigerson Morrison
www.sigersonmorrison.com

Tabitha Simmons
www.tabithasimmons.com

Camilla Skovgaad
www.camillaskovgaard.com

J P Tod's
35 Sloane Street
London SW1X 9LP
Telephone: 0207 235 1321
tods.com

Ugg
39 Long Acre
Covent Garden
London WC2E 9LG
Telephone: 020 7836 5729
www.uggaustralia.co.uk
www.uggaustralia.com

Roger Vivier
www.rogervivier.com

Vivienne Westwood
44 Conduit Street
London W1R 9FB
Telephone: 0207 439 1109
www.viviennewestwood.co.uk

INDEX

Figures in bold refer to main entries.

A
A-POC 51
ACS 52
Adidas 36, 37, 38, 47
Alaïa, Azzedine **72–3**
Atwood, Brian **74–6**

B
Balenciaga 124
Bartley, Luella 37–8
Berardi, Antonio 27, 47, 59, 81
Birkenstock 35, 53, 57, **77**
Blahnik, Manolo 7, 15, 16, 26, 27, 30, 30, 31, 42, 57, 58–9, 63, 67, **78–81**, 151
Boudicca 98
Bourdin, Guy 111
Bowery, Leigh 67
Brody, Neville 83
Buffalo 34, 64, 66

C
Camaleón 82
Camper 21, 53, **82–3**
Céline 37
Chanel 36, 37, 48, **84–5**, 124
Chanel heels 15, 38
Chloé 124
Choo, Jimmy 19, 62, 63, **86–7**
Christian Dior 36
Clark, Nathan 89
Clark, Ossie 81
Clarks 34–5, **89**
Clements Ribeiro 58–9, 79, 81
Colonna, Jean 129
Comme des Garçons 19
Constable, Marcus 98

D
Damier check 37, 38
de Havilland, Terry 34
Desert Boots 35, 89
diamanté-studded shoes 30–1
Dior, Christian 12, 15, 30, 36, 38, 39, 67, 81
Dior denim 38, 39
DIY shoes 50–3
Dolce & Gabbana 19, 35, 42, 63, 67, **92**
Dr Martens 19–20, 65, **90**, 135
Dr Scholl **91**

E
Ellis, Perry 35
evening shoes 97

F
Farhi, Nicole 109
Fendi 23, 24, 37, 38, 39, 48, **93**
Ferragamo, Salvatore 26, 28, 30, 59, 62, **94–7**
flat shoes 18–21
Ford, Tom 16, 17, 67, 102
Free Lance 15, **98–9**

G
Galliano, John 30, 38, 39, 67, 81, 98
Gaultier, Jean-Paul 134
Gina 26, 28, 31, 62–3, 66–7, **100–1**
Gucci 16, 17, 20, 22, 23, 37, 42, 47, 48, 63, 67, **102–5**, 138

H
Halston 30
Hardy, Pierre **106–7**
Harvey Nichols 129
Hemingway, Gerardine 134
Hemingway, Wayne 134
Hermès 36, 37, 48
Hope, Emma 19, **108–9**
Hush Puppies 34–5

J
Jackson, Betty 109
Jacobs, Marc 61
Jesus sandals 20
jewelled shoes 26–31
Jones, Allen 15, 60
Jourdan, Charles 52, **110–11**, 116

K
Karan, Donna 20, 48, 49
Kawakubo, Rei 19, 67
Kélian, Stéphane **112–3**
Kirkwood, Nicholas **114–5**
Kors, Michael 91

L
Lacroix, Christian 34, 124
Lagerfeld, Karl 39, 62, 82, 84, 85, 93, 124
Lauren, Ralph 48
Le Roc, Kele 35
logos 36–9, 93
Louboutin, Christian 60, **116–9**
Louis heels 12–13

M
McCartney, Stella **120–1**
McQueen, Alexander **122–3**
Ménudier, Rodolphe 124–5
Minnie Mouse shoes 60–1
Miu Miu 127
Miyake, Issey 52
Mizrahi, Isaac 91
moccasins 49
Moschino 58, 59
Mugler, Thierry 41
Murkudis, Kostas 129

N
New Balance 47, 52
Nike 38, 39, 44, 45, 47, 49

O
Oehler, Michael 35
Øland, As 51, 53
Olympia, Charlotte **126–7**

P
Perry, Michel 124, **122–3**
pirate boots 156
platform heels 32, 34, 40, 64, 65, 66, 156, 157
Prada 7, 16, 24–5, 32, 47, 48, 49, 52, 63, 93, **130–3**, 130
Prada, Miuccia 130
Prada Sport 38–9, 48, 133
Puma 47

R
Rabanne, Paco 124
Rautureau brothers 98
Red or Dead **134–5**
Repetto **136–7**
Rodriguez, Narciso 77
Rossi, Gianvito 141
Rossi, Sergio 7, 42, 63, **138–4**
Royal Elastics 48

S
Saint Laurent, Yves 111, 155
Sanderson, Rupert 141
Scholl, Dr William 91
Scott, Jeremy 10, 32
Sigerson Morrison
Simmons, Tabitha
Simple 53
Sitbon, Martine 98
Skovgaad, Camilla 148–9
Smith, Paul 20, 109
soles 116, 134
    footbed 77
    platform 97
    wooden 35
Spieth, Angela 35
strap-on heels 10, 32
Sui, Anna 109

T
Tod, J P **150–1**
trainers 44–9
Trippen 35, 53

U
Ugg **152–3**

V
Valentino 30
Valle, Diego delle 150
Versace 42–3, 63, 67
Versace, Donatella 41–2
Versace, Gianni 41, 141
Vivier, Roger 12, 30, 31, 71, **154–5**
Vivo Barefoot 53
Vuitton, Louis 38

W
Wallabee 89
Westwood, Vivienne 42, **156–7**
Worn Again 53

Yamamoto, Yohji 35
Yurkievich, Gaspard 129

ACKNOWLEDGEMENTS

160

The publishers would like to thank the following sources for their kind permission to reproduce the pictures in this book:

t: top, b: bottom, l: left, r:right, tl: top left, tr: top right, bl: bottom left, br: bottom right, bc: bottom centre, bcl: bottom centre left, bcr: bottom centre right.

Courtesy of Acupuncture 49
Courtesy of The Advertising Archives 120, 153
Miles Aldridge for Sergio Rossi 8–9, 10, 139, 140
Robert Allan courtesy of Free Lance 14, 99
All Action/Jonathon Furniss 64tl
Brian Atwood 74-75, 76
Jibby Beane courtesy of Jonathon Gosland 32bl, 156–157
Birkenstock courtesy of Modus Publicity 77
Courtesy of Manolo Blahnik /Manolo Blahnik for Antonio Berardi 42, Gold supplied by 'Chiampesan', Vicenza, Italy 27, 80
© Buffalo Boots Ltd 33, 54–55
Camera Press /Simon Archer 118, 119t /Frederic Farre 73 /Madame Figaro/Frederic Farre 72, /Caroline Menne 119bl /Renaud Wald 106l, 106r, 119br
Courtesy of Camper 21br, 82–83
Pete Canning Photography for Clarks 89tl, 89tr, 89br
Courtesy of Chanel 84l, 85r
Jimmy Choo courtesy of Brower Lewis PR 86bl, 86l, 86–7c, 87r
Christie's Images Ltd 29, 58br
Corbis /Bettmann 20 /WWD/Condé Nast 88tr, 88br
Courtesy of Dolce & Gabbana 92r
Graham Durridge courtesy of Gina 28, 101tr
Christopher Edwick for Free Lance 56, 68–69
Courtesy of Fendi Adele S.R.L. /Karl Lagerfeld 93

Salvatore Ferragamo courtesy of Aurelia PR 26, 94, 95r, 96, 97, 16
Courtesy of Free Lance, Paris 98
Courtesy of Gina 100, 101tl, 101bl
Getty Images 107, 127t, 133l, /AFP 133l /Gamma-Rapho 122, 133r / WireImage 88l, 123l, 126, 127b, 152
Ronald Grant Archive/Batman Returns Warner US 1992 40tr / Barbarella   Panavision France/ Italy 1967 41 /The Red Shoes GFD/The Archers GB 1948 59 / How to Marry a Millionaire TCF US 1953 60
Courtesy of Gucci 22, 47tl, 102tr, 102br, 104, 105b
Courtesy of Hermès (GB) Ltd 36r
Jürgen Holzenleuchter courtesy of Trippen, Germany 35bl, 53bl
Emma Hope courtesy of PH Publicity (photography by Ben Wright) 19br, 21tl, 108r, 109, 158-159 / Paul Smith for Emma Hope 108l
Allen Jones Shoes (1968) 15r
Courtesy of Charles Jourdan 110–11
Courtesy Nicholas Kirkwood 114-115
Ines Van Lamsweerde courtesy of Patrick Cox 70
London Features International Ltd 34tl, 69 /Gie Knaeps 66l /George Pimintel 66r
Courtesy of Christian Louboutin 65b, 116-117
Courtesy of Stella McCartney 121
Niall McInerney 12t, 17, 37, 39r, 43, 84r, 85l, 156l, 157tr, 157b
Courtesy of Rodolphe Ménudier 124-125
Christopher Moore Ltd 2, 15l, 16, 19t, 24, 31, 32r, 35r, 52l, 58l, 79l, 80r, 92tl, 92bl, 97l, 102l, 103, 105t, 134r, 157tl
Sheridan Morley 38b
Courtesy Sigerson Morrison / www. sigersonmorrison.com/ Photographer: Kronus Photo 144-145
Chris Nash courtesy of No Name 44l, 45l

Courtesy of Nike UK 39tl, 45tr, 45br, 46, 48
PA News Photo Library 35tl,
Elaine Perks/Art Direction Mike Bond/Martin Coyne courtesy of As Øland 50l
Courtesy of Michel Perry 128–129
Courtesy of Prada 25, 44tr, 130, 131, 132r, /Alfredo Albertone 132l
Repetto 136
Retna Pictures Ltd /John Spellman 65t
Rex Features /Harry Lamb/BEI 63/ Sipa Press 123r, 137
Courtesy of Sergio Rossi 34br, 40–1c, 138, 141
Catherine Rowlands 12b, /Bouddica 13
Courtesy of Rupert Sanderson 142–143
Jonathon Sands courtesy of Red Or Dead 134l, 135
Dr Scholl courtesy of SSL International 91
Matthew Shave 1, 47r
Courtesy Tabitha Simmons 146–147
Courtesy Camilla Skovgaard 148–149
William Taylor courtesy of Adidas UK 36l /Manolo Blahnik 30, 78, 79r, 80l, Jimmy Choo 18 /Patrick Cox 61 /Fendi 23, 38t /R Griggs Group Ltd (Dr Martens AirWair) 90 /As Øland 50r, 53tr, /Yves Saint Laurent 154r, 155l
Courtesy of Tod's 150–151
Topham Picturepoint 155r
Courtesy of Trippen, Germany 52-3t
Courtesy of Yves Saint Laurent /(AW 1965) 154l

Every effort has been made to acknowledge correctly and contact the source and/or copyright holder of each picture, and Carlton Books Limited apologizes for any unintentional errors or omissions which will be corrected in future editions of this book.

Thank you to all the PR companies, fashion houses and shoe designers who provided information and visuals for this book. Thanks to Ruth at Camper, Paola at Dolce & Gabbana, as well as to Sophia for always being high on heels, and to Jo for never letting a broken heel slow her down. I am also grateful to Venetia Penfold for her enthusiasm, Zia Mattocks for her patience and to Barbara Zuñiga and Catherine Costelloe for their creativity and vision.

Tamsin Blanchard